Measuring

KEY STAGE TWO

PHOTOCOPIABLES

impact

MATHS HOMEWORK

Published by Scholastic Ltd,
Villiers House,
Clarendon Avenue,
Leamington Spa,
Warwickshire CV32 5PR

© 1994 Scholastic Ltd
3 4 5 6 7 8 9   7 8 9 0 1 2

UNIVERSITY OF
NORTH LONDON

Activities by the IMPACT Project
at the University of North London,
collated and rewritten by Ruth
Merttens and Ros Leather

Editor Noel Pritchard
Assistant editor Sophie Jowett
Designer Rita Storey (Storeybooks)
Series designer Anna Oliwa
Illustrations Roger Fereday
Cover illustration Roger Wade Walker

Designed using Aldus Pagemaker
Processed by Salvo Print and Design
Artwork by Pages Bureau, Leamington Spa
Printed in Great Britain by Ebenezer Baylis,
Worcester

British Library Cataloguing-in-Publication Data
A catalogue record for this book is
available from the British Library.

ISBN 0-590-53157-3

Measuring

CONTENTS

Measuring

impact
CONTENTS

impact
INTRODUCTION

This series of IMPACT books is designed to help you run a non-traditional homework scheme. Through the use of take- home maths activities, children can share maths with a parent/carer in the context of the home. The results of these activities then feed back into the classwork at school. IMPACT works through the following processes.

● Teachers plan their maths for the next few weeks as usual and consider which parts might usefully be done at home.

● Teachers look through selected activities that fit in with their planning.

● The activities are photocopied and sent home with the children every week or fortnight.

● The results of each activity are brought back to school by the children and form part of the following week's classwork.

In practice this process will be slightly different in each classroom and in each school. Teachers may adapt it to fit their own way of working and the ethos of the school in which they work. Most schools send out IMPACT activities fortnightly, although some do send it weekly. There is some evidence to suggest that weekly activities get a slightly better response and help to raise standards more effectively than fortnightly, but this is not conclusive. The important point is that each teacher should feel comfortable with how often the IMPACT activities are used in his/her class.

Planning

When you, the teacher, are looking at your work and deciding what maths, roughly speaking, you plan to be doing over the next few weeks, all that is necessary is to consider which parts may usefully be done or practised at home. It is helpful if, over a period of time, a range of activities are chosen in order to vary the mathematical experience in the home and the type and amount of follow-up required in class.

The activities tend to fall into three broad categories:

● Activities which practise a skill – these are useful in that they can be followed up in the routine classwork the children are doing. They must be carefully selected by the teacher according to the level of the children.

● Activities which collect data – these lead into work on data-handling and representation.

● Activities in which the children measure something – this produces an object or some measurements to be used later in class.

The activities in this book are divided into sections under the maths topic headings: length, area, weight, volume and capacity, money, time and temperature. Teachers' notes relating to the individual activities are featured on pages six to ten. A page of squared paper is included on page 127 and can be photocopied to accompany activities as required. Details of the coverage of the curricula in Scotland and Northern Ireland are given on page 128.

Working with parents

It is important for the success of IMPACT that the activities taken home are seen by the parents to be maths. We always suggest, at least until IMPACT is up and running and parents' confidence in it is well established, that activities are chosen which have a clearly mathematical purpose. Save the more 'wacky' activities until later! You will get a much better response if parents believe that what they are doing is maths.

Each activity contains a note to parents which explains the purpose of the activity and how they can best help. The IMPACT activities should be accompanied by an IMPACT diary, enabling parents and children to make their comments.

The diaries provide a mechanism by means of which an efficient parent-teacher dialogue is established. Through these diaries, which last up to two years depending upon the frequency of the IMPACT tasks, teachers obtain valuable feedback both about children's performance on the specific maths tasks and about the tasks themselves. Parents are able to alert the teacher to weaknesses and strengths and nothing about the child's performance in maths comes as a surprise at the end of the year or when statutory assessments are administered. The diaries are a crucial part of this homework scheme.

Making the most of IMPACT

The quickest way to reduce the number of children who share maths at home is to ignore or be negative about the work that they bring back into school. When the children come running into the classroom, tripping over the string which went twice round their cat, it is difficult to welcome them all individually but it is crucial that the activities done at home are followed up in classwork. The nature and type of this follow-up work depends very much upon the nature of the activity, and specific suggestions are made in the teachers' notes. However, some general points apply:

● Number activities, such as games, can often be repeated in a more formalised way in the classwork. For example, if the children have been playing a dice game, throwing two dice and adding the totals, they can continue to do this in the classroom, but this time they can record all the 'sums' in their maths books. This applies to any skills-practice activity.

● Data-collecting activities, of any description, need to be followed up by allowing the children to work together in small groups to collate, analyse and represent their joint data. This will inevitably involve children in a discussion as to how their data was obtained, and any problems they encountered while obtaining it.

● If the children have made or measured something at home, the information or the object needs to be used as part of the resulting classwork. This will not be too difficult since this type of activity is selected by the teacher.

The implication of this is that it is wise to select a variety of activities to send home. No teacher wants to drown in data, nor do they want all the IMPACT activities to result in more routine number work. Some activities generate lots of follow-up while others simply require a minimum – sometimes just a discussion about who won and who lost, and how many times people played the game.

Many of the activities can lead to an attractive display or enable the teacher to make a class book. Such a book does not have to be 'grand'. It can be simply five or six sheets large sheets of sugar paper folded in the middle and stitched/stapled with the children's work mounted inside it. The children love these books, and they make a fine record of their work. An IMPACT display board in the school entrance hall gives parents a sense that their work at home is appreciated.

Teachers' Notes

All these activities provide opportunities for children to use and apply their mathematical skills outside the context of the classroom. This means that every activity will address some aspects of the 'Using and applying' part of the Programme of Study (was AT1). Commonly children may be expected to do the following whilst sharing IMPACT activity:
● use and apply mathematics in real-life problems, and in situations where they are exploring the mathematics itself,
● think their own way through a problem, argue and justify their reasons,
● develop their own strategies and discuss these with others,
● follow instructions, provide a series of instructions of their own where appropriate, and
● discuss and analyse their results.

In all of these skills, mathematical language plays a very important role. Sharing IMPACT children are constantly using and developing their language skills in mathematics. The evidence from OFSTED and other reports now clearly demonstrates that IMPACT can have a marked effect in helping children succeed in using and applying their mathematical skills.

The activities in this book also address aspects of the Programme of Study for Shape, Space and Measures, and also some of the measurement parts of the Number. This book utilises the following skills:

● selecting and using common standard units of length, area, volume, weight and temperature,
● making direct and indirect comparisons using standard and non-standard units of length, area, volume, capacity, weight and time,
● making suitable estimates of a variety of different measurements,
● relating the circumference of a round object to its diameter,
● selecting the appropriate coins to use in any one circumstance, and understanding their relative values, and
● utilising with some accuracy a variety of different measuring instruments and scales.

LENGTH

Tall and fat When the children bring their drawings into class, they can work in groups and put them in order of height, then in order of fatness. Are the orders the same? Measure around some things in class and talk about the difficulties involved.

Feet in cm The children can compare feet measurements. How many feet can they fit on one metre? What is the difference between the longest foot and the shortest?

Hand and wrist When the children bring in their wrist measurement, discuss who was closest in their estimate. How many centimetres out were they? What is the difference between the longest and the shortest wrist measurement? Between the longest and the shortest handspan? Can they make a graph to show their results?

Metre estimates NB Each child will need a piece of string exactly one metre long. When they bring in their lists, ask them to collect their things into two large sets – things longer than one metre, and things shorter than one metre.

How long? NB Each child will need a piece of string exactly one metre long. When the children bring their measures

back into class they can make up two sets – one of the objects which were between 2 and 3 metres long, and one which contains anything which was between 3 and 4 metres. Mark out the perimeter of the classroom in metres.

Standard units NB Each child will need a piece of string exactly one metre long. The children can sort the things they have found into sets under the different headings given on the sheet. They can then find things in the classroom under the same headings.

Metre me NB Each child will need a metre strip with centimetre markings. Encourage them to display their scale drawings in order of height.

Metre game NB Each child will need a piece of string exactly one metre long. The children can play this game in class. They can then try to find objects they would measure using a decimetre, objects that they would measure using a centimetre, and objects that they would measure using a metre. This will help them to choose an appropriate unit.

Body lengths The children will require a metre rule for this activity. They can compare lengths and make a graph representing each length by squares on t

Jumps The children can compare their jumps and work in groups to put them in order. The intention is to lead into a discussion on why footsteps are not a very good way to measure – and to sggest the need for standard units.

Aeroplanes NB Each child will need a metre strip with centimetre markings. The children can compare the distances their planes flew. Are any of them very unlikely? What was the furthest/least far? What was the difference in centimetres between the two? Can they make a chart showing the distances – with planes down the left-hand side and the distances shown as a line stretching out from the

plane horizontally? What scale will they use for this?

Armspans and heights Each child will need a metre strip with centimetre markings. They can share their findings. Which people in the survey are square, i.e. they come out with an armspan that is the same as their height? Which people are vertical oblongs – height longer than armspans? Which are horizontal oblongs – armspans longer than height?

Body measurement The children can share their findings back in class. They can measure their handspan and cubit using centimetres then work out differences between their own and other people's in centimetres. Why does the relationship between the two stay fairly constant?

Long numbers NB You will need to give the children the piece of paper to use, otherwise all their numbers will be different sizes! They can measure their strings in centimetres – which number is the longest/shortest? Can they double the length of the string and then use it to draw a number which is twice as long? Is it then twice as big?

Diplodocus measures Would the diplodocus be able to stand in the school playground? Would he fit in the school hall? How big were his feet? Can they make a series of footprints to go across the school hall? This leads on to lots of measuring and calculating.

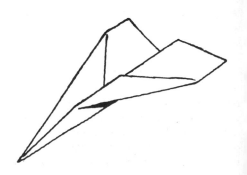

Long jump The children can make a chart of all their jumps. The chart can have small drawings of them down the left-hand column and a line representing the length of their jump running from left to right (which will need to be calculated according to a suitable scale).

Paper chains NB It is important to give the children the piece of paper to use – if this is brightly coloured then you can use the resulting chains to make a wonderful display.

Lengthy plans Perhaps the children can work out the area of floor which doesn't have any furniture on it. This may be about the same, proportionally, whatever this size of the room.

Timing races The children can compare their times. Do they think some times are more plausible than others? What could have affected the accuracy of the measurements? Can they produce a strip exactly 50m long by sticking shorter (coloured) sections together?

Eyesight test NB Each child will need a metre strip with centimetre markings. They can share their boards and try them out on each other. Are some more suitable for the person being tested to stand further away than others? In groups, can the children make one board which they think will actually do the job well? What are the distances involved These need to be exact in order to obtain proper criteria for what counts as standard eyesight testing.

Wrap around The children can discuss what they found out. Hopefully they will all have discovered that the diameter always goes three times into the circumference. This can then be used as the basis of a discussion about pi.

Around and about Each child will need a metre strip with centimetre markings in order for them to do this activity. The children can check the accuracy of their measurements using this trick – multiply the diameter by three and this should give the circumference measurement. Let them check this out to see if it works. This will lead into a discussion about the relationship between the diameter and the circumference – i.e. pi.

Millimetre money NB Each child will need a ruler with millimetres. The children can make a chart of all the coins of the realm showing their diameters in millimetres. They can discuss how difficult it was to measure some of the coins, e.g. the 50p, and why. Suppose each coin's diameter were to be multiplied by four. What size would the coin then become? Can they draw some of these 'big' coins? Suppose the diameter were multiplied by eight?

Miles away The children can discuss the relationship between miles and kilometres and they can draw a conversion graph. The Fibonacci sequence can also be plotted on the graph as a series of coordinates. Compare the two lines. The children can also discuss converting from other imperial units to S1 units – from gallons to litres (e.g. for petrol).

Car lengths NB Each child will need a metre strip with centimetre markings. The children can share their car lengthsand categorise them into small, medium and large. They can perhaps draw a picture of their car to scale using the length measurement.

String cuts NB Each child will need a ruler with millimetres. They can play this game in class. It can get pretty exciting and sometimes quite fine judgements need to be made! At the end they can estimate how long all their pieces of string are when put together.

Thick pages NB Each child will need a ruler with millimetres. The children can compare answers. These may vary surprisingly, not only because they have made errors but also because they have chosen books with thinner pages or thick pages. They can compare answers and work out what a book with one million pages would look like.

Take away The children can do subtraction and division sums with these standard units in class. If they appear to be having a hard time visualising what these lengths look like, they can play the game with lengths of string which they measure and cut.

Cassette lengths The children can compare lengths and methods. Which ways do they think are likely to have produced the most accurate results? Are the answers similar – or are some wildly different? Bring in an old cassette tape which the children can actually spread out and measure!

Walk about The children can compare their estimates. First of all, establish an order of magnitude. Do the estimates all sound realistic – or are some way off-beam? What are the parameters for this exercise? Once these are established, encourage the children to study each other's charts and look at the places where they may have disagreed or forgotten something. Can they make a graph of the distance they all walk on a typical day?

Faster, faster NB Each child will need a metre strip with centimetre markings. The children can compare their speeds. Who moves fastest/slowest? Did it make any difference how long their course was? Discuss what difference this might have made – a longer race is run more slowly. Were they quicker crawling or hopping?

Speed signs The children can compare all their signs. Which ones were common? Did anyone find a sign that no one else had seen? Were all the signs aimed at cars? What would a sign aimed at cyclists say? What about a speed sign aimed at pedestrians? What are the units used in measuring speed? Make a list of these, alongside a display of the signs.

AREA

Tin area The children could discuss how they found their area. How many methods did they try? They could find half the label area. How do they find half? How many ways can they find to display this? Will all the shapes be rectangles?

Box area Children could work in groups to find the areas of different boxes. Can they investigate a quicker method of finding the area of their box?
Metre of fun Using prepared metre squares, the children could work in small groups to discover if all the pupils' shoes will fit on to a square metre. How many dinner plates will fit on to a square metre?

Window panes The children could investigate making different regular shaped windows with the same area. Are there some areas that allow more shapes to be made?

Jigsaw areas The children could work in small groups and make complete squares using the various fractions. These could be arranged in a variety of regular shapes, each showing an area of 144cm.

Decimetre boxes The children can investigate the surface area of various arrangements of four boxes/eight boxes. Which arrangement has the largest/smallest area?

Letter areas Groups of children could arrange their letters in various orders, for example perimeter, area, height and width. Has the tallest letter the biggest area?

Toy area This activity could be extended to finding the total surface area of other small objects. These could be Multilink models of numbers or letters.

Handy area The children can cut out their 'hands' and explain how they calculated the area. Which squares were difficult to count? How did they decide which squares not to count? They could arrange their hands in area order – do their perimeters follow the same order?

The big screen The children could work in groups with their decimetre squares. How many different arrangements with an area of 12 decimetre squares can they make? Are the perimeters all the same?

Perimeters The children can explore the relationship between area and perimeter in their classwork. What is the best shape if they want to get the smallest possible perimeter and the largest area?

Enlarging a picture Display the children's pictures and discuss how much larger the area is in the second one. They need to see that if they double the length of a side, the area is quadrupled.

Boxing clever There are many possible solutions – the children should discuss them and agree that each works. Have they remembered to add the lid? Which of their possible boxes has the largest volume?

Surfaces Discuss the different strategies that children used in their attempts to solve this problem. Which do they feel were the best ways of finding the surface area of an arm?

Circular hunt Children can look at their different circles. When they put them all together, can they see a relationship between the radius and the area? Once they have established that there is a constant ratio between the radius squared and the area, they can begin to work out *pi*.

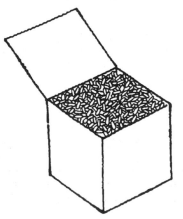

Secret garden The main concern here is how the children approached the problem rather than the correct answer. Clearly the best shape is a circle if the friend is to minimise fencing, but several children may suggest as near a square as possible because they are working on rectangles.

VOLUME AND CAPACITY

Handful of water The children could hold a group competition measuring their handfuls with 5ml medicine spoons. Teams could be ordered by their totals and the differences calculated.

Bath count-up The children could group themselves by type of measure (litres, pints, quarts, gallons). Discuss which measures are most suitable for large quantities and where these measures are used (cooking, petrol, milk).

Guess along The children could work in pairs to convert the medicine spoonfuls into millilitres. The measurements could be added to make litre measures, for example, two mugs and three cups hold one litre.

100ml and counting Record the capacity of small containers using 5ml spoon drawings to represent the totals as a pictogram. These could be ordered and differences calculated. Can they find containers that will total 1000ml (1 litre)?

Bathroom look out Encourage the children to bring empty containers to school. These can be ordered for capacity. This will also help them to realise that the shape can vary but the capacity can be the same.

Make a litre Ask the children to bring a variety of containers to school. When labels have been removed they can try to order their containers for capacity. Investigate how may hold more than a litre – are there any smaller measures that add up to equal 1 litre?

How much do they hold? The children could work in groups to make cylinders

which have a volume the same as the fat cylinder or the thin cylinder.

Tin volume The children could estimate and measure the volume of different containers.

Litres and pints The children may like to investigate the information displayed at petrol stations and attempt to work out a conversion table showing the relationship between gallons and litres.

Drawer measure The children could work in pairs to make cubic decimetres. They could investigate how many different shapes could be made with a set of number cubes.

Largest cube The children can compare their cubes. How have they elected to solve the problem? Has anyone produced an unusual solution? Working in groups, using lentils or rice the children can find out how much their boxes will hold. Measuring the capacity of these will enable them to find a means of categorising them for display.

Boxes of rice The children can share their ways of solving this problem and compare their boxes. How many different shapes are there? What are the dimensions? Find the volume – by calculation – using a calculator if necessary, of all the boxes. Do they have the same volume? They should.

Brick pretence The children can compare answers to see if there is a generally agreed solution. They will then need to make this 'brick' out of Multilink or Centicubes and count the numbers for themselves. Encourage them to explore this further – what would happen with a brick of a different size?

Balloon difference NB Ensure each child has a balloon so that they can compare their findings. Did all the children find the same answer? If not, what might account for these differences? Discuss the margin of error to be expected – is 10% reasonable or not? Perhaps the children can find the

volume and capacity of something else where these may differ radically – a thermos flask, or a hot water bottle.

Calculate or measure The children can discuss why the two ways of obtaining a volume produced different answers – if they did! How close were most chidren's answers? What do they feel accounted for the differences? Which way of working out the volume do they feel was the best, and why would one way be better in some circumstances? (for example, if the box was solid!). Talk about percentage errors, and the way of measuring which should produce the least error.

Pet weights The children could sort and order their weights then work in groups to display the data collected using different methods.

Weighing ten This activity will involve the children in discussions and calculations, for example if they weigh ten potatoes and divide the total by ten will they obtain the weight of any one potato? The children could work in groups to check answers and find average weights of uneven objects.

Race to one kilo The children should weigh kilo bags of different substances, such as cornflakes, feathers, stones, soil. Children could estimate a kilo beforehand. You could make your own weights and have the children working in groups to investigate the weights. What is the minimum number of weights required for accurate measuring to one kilo?

Weigh a handful The children could estimate the weight of a handful of different substances. The substances could be ordered in weight. Does everyone have the same order? Which substances weigh the most/least? Why?

Cup of difference The children could order their differences on a chart and illustrate this with the substances that they used. How can the variations be explained?

TIME

Time to play When the children bring their timelines back into class, they can study them and collate their information. What times of day did they eat? How long did they spend eating? What was the longest time anyone spent shopping? What was the least? The information they collect can be displayed on a series of charts or graphs.

Record breakers The children can compare their times. Who is a slow coach/ speedy? Talk about different times of day – are they slower in the morning than in the evening? They can make a chart of the different lengths of time they each took. Discuss bedtimes and getting-up times. How long do they sleep each day?

Timing times The children can record times in class on both digital and analogue clocks. Talk about the numbers of minutes in an hour and the number of seconds in a minute. Include the 24 hour clock since some digital watches work on this.

All in a muinute The children can compare their times. Who manages to do the most/least? Make a chart for each activity to show the amounts completed in the minute and the numbers of children with these amounts. Find other events they can do in the classroom in one minute!

In the blink of an eye The children can compare their times. Who took the longest? Who took the shortest? They can make a chart for each activity showing the lengths of time taken and the numbers of chidren with each length of time.

TV watch? The children can work out the differences between their times. Who took longest/shortest? Discuss programme times and radio times. Are most programmes half an hour or longer? Why do they there are more programmes of a certain length?

A watched clock Collect all the different times and put them into sets according to what hour of the day they fall under – all the times between 8.00 and 9.00 am can go in one set, all those between 9.00 and 10.00 am in another, etc. Talk about how many minutes there are in an hour, and what times are nearest to being 'o'clock'.

Year clock The children can make one large colourful year clock which can be displayed with their individual clocks around it. They can collate their own personal information to make the large class year clock.

Chinese year signs Children can draw their year animal and display the decorated names of all the people who were born as that animal. This will involve collating all the information that they have brought back home. Talk about how long ago different years were. What is the number of years between 1986 and this year? Make a year timeline for the children to count along.

What day is it? Have the children all got the same answere where appropriate? Do they agree with each other? Look up some other days of importance in class – beginning and end of term, sports days, and so on, then make a display with days and drawings of them in sets labelled by the names of the days of the week.

Calendar count up This activity can be used in the same way as *What day is it?*, above.

Round the clock The children can help each other to calculate their total amount of time spent eating. It will help to discuss how many minutes long each interval is – especially those which go over the hour. Concentrate on just the minutes where it is possible.

Ticking clocks The children can play this game in class. They can move the big hand five minutes at a time and write down the time on each move. Can they write the time in digital and in words? Count in fives around the clock with the whole class and make a class clock.

Second time Ask the chldren to use a one metre pendulum to time events in class. How many seconds does it take them to throw a six on a dice? How many seconds to write their name ten times?

Judge of time Try this activity in class, making the children all shut their eyes, saying 'Go' and then telling them to put their hand up silently when they think one minute has passed. When they have their hand up, they may open their eyes, but not before. Who is closest/least close? Are most not estimating long enough? Why do they think this is? The children can then collate their results by putting them into sets according to how close they were.

Freezing cold Compare the drying times for various garments. The children can draw the different garments and then write out the drying times and display them. Help them to work out the intervals if they know the starting point and the finishing point.

Heartbeat How much do the children's results vary? Discuss which seems to be the more accurte figure – the one taken over six seconds and multiplied by ten, or the one taken over one minute. Talk about the problem of multiplying any error. You can make a chart of pulse rates. Can they take their pulse after doing exercise?

Washing times How long did different materials take to dry? Use examples of different materials – wool, cotton, nylon, lycra – and display the drying times beside them. Help the children to work out the interval from the starting time and the finishing time. A timeline – with hours and minutes arranged in a line – can be useful. Suggest they focus on the minutes, rather than the hour. Especial help will be needed with any that go across an 'o'clock'.

Life times Working in groups the children can compare their strips. Help them to understand that the length of these represents a number of years. They can then create a block graph showing how many strips of each length they have collected altogether.

Family history The children can collect all their results and make one enormous timeline with the events of interest on it. They will need to talk about establishing how long ago something was, or the number of years between particular events. It helps arithmetic if they only look at the last two digits of the year.

Christmas time You will need a globe to explain how Lola seems to be going backwards in time! She starts in Melbourne at 20.00 after Christmas dinner. She then travels on the plane for 16 hours, having a second Christmas meal on the plane somewhere over the Pacific, also on Christmas Day. After landing, she then drives to her family and has a third Christmas dinner. Can the children work out a similar story? What happens if the dateline is crossed going the other way?

TV survey The children can share their results to see if they tally. They may have chosen different days and you will need to discuss why this might make a difference. Some of the children can work out the proportion of new programmes givien the overall figure for the number of hours on air. They can all discuss which channel gives most priority to the news, given the total broadcasting hours they have.

Time leaks The children can work in groups testing and improving their timers. Which ones time exactly one minute? When they are satisfied with their timers, they can time themselves doing as many sums as possible in one minute.

Seasonal times The children can compare their thoughts. There will probably be some discrepancies and it would be useful to have the official hours of daylight figures for summer and winter handy to settle any disputes. The children can make a graph of the number of hours of daylight for each month. Talk about why the hours change.

Century times This activity can be followed up by asking the children to work out how many of their ages put together would make a century. They can also think about what year it was when they were born, how they would write that year, how they would write the year a century before that, and how they would write the year a century after they were born.

Millions of seconds Discuss how the children would write the numbers involved in words – much harder than figures! This is good for their understanding of large numbers. They can also work out how many days of their life they have spent asleep. How many minutes have they spent in their life eating, watching TV or playing?

MONEY

Coin collect The children can play a version of this game in pairs in class, where they have to write down the coins they take, add them up and write the answer in their maths book. It is also useful to discuss the probability aspects – how likely is it that all the coins will fall heads or tails? What is the chance of one coin falling heads or tails?

Coin threesome The children can draw or write all their different items and sort them into sets according to the amount – everything between 20p and 30p in this set, everything between 30p and 40p in that set, and so on. They can discuss whether an amount, e.g. 22p, can be made using more than one combination of three coins. What combinations of threee coins were most popular, and why?

Change for 50p Children need to do lots of work on the giving of change. Encourage them to count on, rather thn performing a written two-line subtraction sum. Display and talk about the different amounts of change you get for different coins, e.g. change for 4p from 20p is 16p, from 50p is 46p.

Big money The children can discuss and share their chosen items then draw them and work out how much it would cost to buy all the items on their table. Would they get change out of £5 if they bought all the cheap ones? Discuss which items represent value for money and what this means.

Noteworthy The children can collect all the things they have managed to find that can be bought for their note and display these in sets according to the value of the note. How much would they need to spend if they bought all the sweet foods in the food category? How much if they bought the fizzy drinks? Lots of arithmetic can stem from this activity.

Score of coins Encourage the children to play the game in class, especially those who did not get to play it at home. They can then formalise some of the arithmetic by throwing the dice, adding the scores and writing down any coin they get in their maths book. They must keep a running score until they have collected five of the six possible coins under £1!

Change for £1 This activity can be used in much the same way as Change for 50p.

Easy change Discuss how much the children think each journey would cost and the care that bus drivers take to have certain coins ready for giving change. The children can then do a great deal of arithmetic based on buying tickets with different coins.

Close approximation It is very useful for children to practise rounding up and rounding down – this helps to develop their understanding of place value as well as aiding estimation. In class, they can make up shopping lists for each other, and then round them up and down and see if the new list added up is any different from the old one!

Price wise The children can share their findings with one another and perhaps make a graph of the different prices – item type against variation in amount from cheapest to most expensive. They can work out which items are 'reasonably priced' and what they think this means. Perhaps you can mount a display of 'Today's best buys'!

Biscuit value The children can discuss how much each of their biscuits cost Were some more definitely value for money than others? Do they think that some should be cheaper? Perhaps they can display the results of their survey on a graph or chart?

Shopping basket survey This activity can lead to a phenomenal amount of follow-up work in class. The children can try to calculate the cost of the very cheapest 'shopping basket' of essentials by collating all their information and choosing the cheapest items. They can make a graph of the items in the basket along with the number who chose that particular item for their basket, e.g. if 25 people put margarine as essential, it gets a coloum of 25 on the graph.

How much do I need? The children can work in small groups and discuss how they planned their spending. Which decisions do they feel are purely personal, and which are made out of necessity? Could you get away with spending nothing on clothes? For how long could they do this?

Realm count up Give the children the correct answer and check that everyone agreed with this. What about in other currencies? What do all the French or American coins/notes add up to? Is it roughly the same amount? There is a great deal of maths – conversion graphs, exchange and so on, that can continue from this activity.

Rich uncle Give the children the solution to this problem. Can they now make up their own problems, like this for other children to solve? Warn them that the difficulty is that their problem must have *only one unique solution* – you must not be able to make up the amount following the criteria given in any way other than the one intended!

How much is a cornflake? The children can compare their results. Which children chose the same cereals? Did they get comparable amounts? What about comparing the cost of one cornflake with that of other cereals? It may come as something of a shock to some children to realise how many more times as expensive some of the more fancy cereals are than the basics! Make a graph showing the prices for one bowlful of each cereal.

Tricky question One billion is written 1,000,000,000,000,000. It will cost £1.30 since it has 13 numerals. The children can make numerals out of card and create really large numbers out of them for display. Can they read out these large numbers?

TEMPERATURE

Person temperatures The children can compare the units used by the different thermometers. Do they all use the same? What are the possible units for measuring temperature? They should also make a graph of their own body temperatures – these will vary slightly. Talk about the variations.

Weather search Talk about the different units used to measure temperature. Which units used to be used in Britain? Which units are used nowadays? What is the temperature range within which British temperature varies? Discuss what it means when the temperature is a negative number. The children can use their understanding of this situation to help them do some work on negative numbers.

Note that much of the resulting material from these activities can be used to create attractive classroom displays.

Tall and fat

YOU WILL NEED: a toy; a pencil; scissors and some string.

● Choose one of your toys, such as a doll, a dinosaur or a teddy. How tall do you think it is? How fat? Write down your estimates.

My estimates:

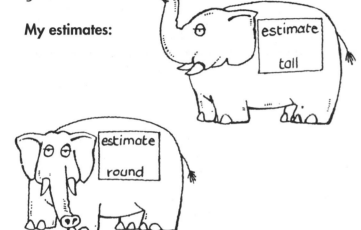

● Now draw round your toy on a piece of paper.

● Cut out the 10 centimetre strip at the bottom of the page and use the strip to measure how many centimetres tall your toy is. Write the measurements on your drawing.

● Now use a piece of string or wool to wind around your toy's tummy just one time. Cut it so it fits round exactly once.

● Stretch the string out and measure it. This is how fat your toy is!

● Write this down beside your drawing.

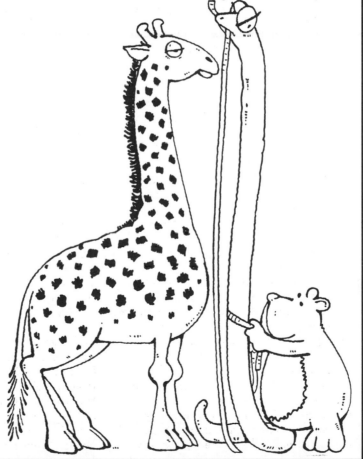

| 0 | 5 | 10 |

Dear Parent or Carer

This activity will give your child practice in measuring things and using the standard unit of the centimetre. It is helpful that one of the lengths is a perimeter because we shall be talking about the distance round things in class.

_____and
child

_____
helper(s)

_____

did this activity together

Dear Parent or Carer

This activity helps children to learn to measure. This is a skill which requires practice. Remind them to line up the heel with the beginning of the strip.

_____and

child

_____

helper(s)

_____

did this activity together

Feet in centimetres

YOU WILL NEED: the 20 centimetre strip at the bottom of this page; paper and scissors.

● Cut out the strip and, if possible, stick it on to a piece of card. This will help strengthen it.

● Now measure the foot lengths of all your family and friends. (You may need to make 2 strips if their feet are big!)

● Ask each person to take off their shoe. (They can keep their stockings or socks on.)

● Ask them to stand on your strip – with the edge of their heel on the zero end. How long is their foot?

● Write their name on the list and the length of their foot in centimetres beside it.

● Measure as many people as you can. Don't forget yourself!

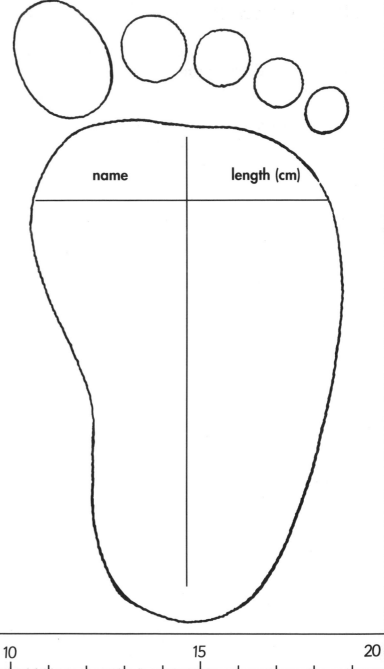

name	length (cm)

0   5   10   15   20

impact MATHS HOMEWORK

Hand and wrist

YOU WILL NEED: a pencil and some string.

Which is longer – your handspan or the distance around your wrist?

● Estimate how many centimetres long you think they each are. Which do you think is longer? Write down your estimates.

Guesses: Wrist ....

Handspan ....

● Now measure your handspan by stretching your hand out along the centimetre strip at the bottom of the page. Write down the answer.

My handspan is .... **cm**

● Measure your wrist using a piece of string. Wrap it around your wrist so that the ends just touch. How many centimetres long is it? Write down the answer.

My wrist is .... **cm**

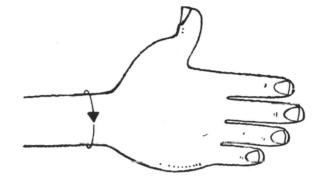

● How close were you?

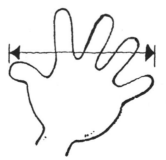

```
0                5                10                15                20
```

_____and
child

_____
helper(s)

_____
did this activity together

_____and

child

_____

helper(s)

_____

did this activity together

Metre estimates

YOU WILL NEED: a piece of string exactly 1 metre long.

● Look around your home and find 5 things that are just longer (or taller) than your piece of string.

● Find 5 things that are just shorter.

● Write them down in the chart.

longer	shorter

impact MATHS HOMEWORK

How long?

YOU WILL NEED: a piece of string exactly 1 metre long.

● Look around your home. (You can look indoors and outdoors if you wish.)

● Can you see something which is between 2 and 3 metres long?

● Write down its name or draw it.

● Write down approximately how long you think it is, for example 2.5 metres.

● Now use your metre string to measure it. Were you right?

● Can you see anything that is between 3 and 4 metres long? (This may have to be outside!)

● If you can, try to measure it!

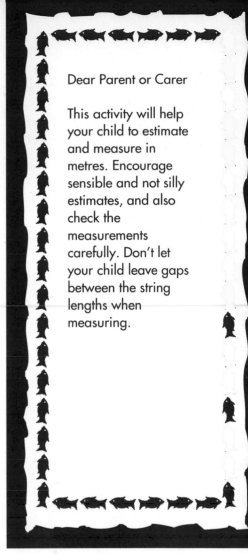

Dear Parent or Carer

This activity will help your child to estimate and measure in metres. Encourage sensible and not silly estimates, and also check the measurements carefully. Don't let your child leave gaps between the string lengths when measuring.

_____and

child

_____

helper(s)

_____

did this activity together

I.M. MARSH LIBRARY LIVERPOOL L17 6BD
TEL. 0151 231 5216/5299

Dear Parent or Carer

This activity will help your child to understand and to use metres, decimetres and centimetres. It will help to demonstrate the relationship between these lengths.

_____and

child

_____

helper(s)

_____

did this activity together

Standard units

YOU WILL NEED: a pencil; a piece of string 1 metre long and the decimetre strip at the bottom of this page.

● Find 3 things longer than 1 metre.

● Find 3 things shorter than 1 metre but longer than 1 decimetre.

● Find 3 things shorter than 1 decimetre but longer than 1 centimetre.

● Write them down in the boxes below.

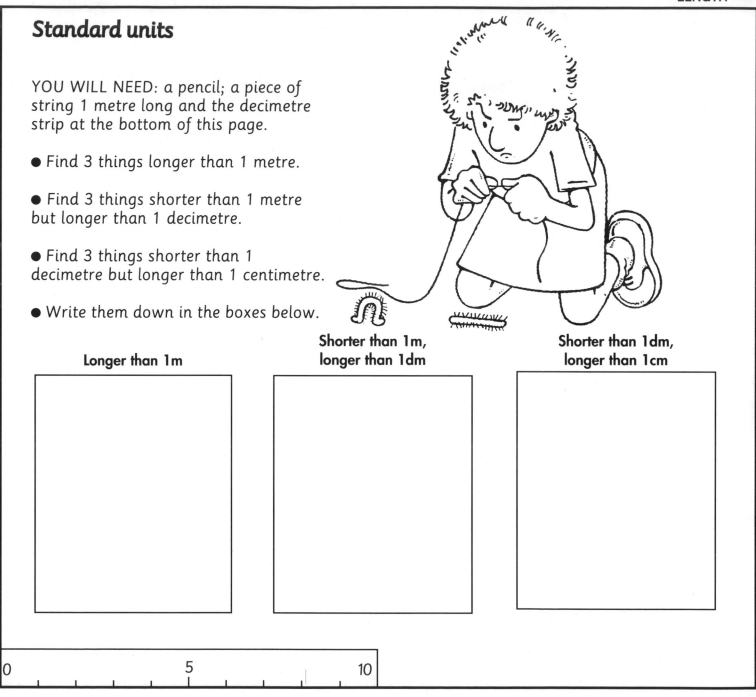

Longer than 1m

Shorter than 1m, longer than 1dm

Shorter than 1dm, longer than 1cm

0   5   10

impact MATHS HOMEWORK

Metre me

YOU WILL NEED: squared paper;
a piece of string 1 metre in length;
a ruler; a pencil and 2 books.

● Use your metre string and ruler to measure yourself and someone else in your family. Try to be accurate.

● Lie down on the floor. Ask your partner to put a book at your head and a book at your feet.

● Stand up carefully, being sure not to move the books. Use your metre string and ruler to measure how tall you are in centimetres. Write down your answer.

I am .... cm tall

● Draw yourself on one of the strips of squared paper below. First of all, make it the right height by counting one square for every 10 centimetres of your height. So if you are 134cm, you draw a line at just over 13 squares high. Then draw yourself so that the top of your head touches the line and your feet touch the bottom of the strip. This is a scale drawing!

● Do the same thing for someone else in your home.

Dear Parent or Carer

This activity is quite demanding because it involves the child in producing a scale drawing of themselves and someone else. We shall use these drawings in class for further work on scale and measurement.

_____and
child

_____
helper(s)

did this activity together

Dear Parent or Carer

This activity is designed to help to reinforce the notions of metres, decimetres and centimetres, and the relationship between them. Talk to your child about these different units as you play.

_____and

child

_____

helper(s)

_____

did this activity together

Metre game

YOU WILL NEED: a dice; a piece of string 1 metre long; 20 decimetre strips (use the one at the bottom of the page to make others the same length); 20 centimetre squares and 2 large boards like the one shown on this page.

● Place all of the measuring strips in a central pile.

● Take it in turns to throw the dice twice.

● Add the scores together and collect that number of centimetres from the pile.

● Place them in the right column on your board.

● When you have 10 centimetres (cm) you can swap them for 1 decimetre (dm).

● Keep playing and collect the measuring strips. When you eventually have 10dm you can swap them for the metre string! The first player to collect the metre string is the winner.

m	dm	cm

0   5   10

impact MATHS HOMEWORK

Body lengths

YOU WILL NEED: a ball of string or wool; a tape measure and some scissors.

How long a piece of string would it take to go right round your body?

● Lie down on the floor with your arms and legs spread out.

● Ask your partner to lay the string all the way around the outline of your body.

● Cut off the string to the right length.

How many metres and centimetres long is the string?

My string is [ ] **long**

I.M. MARSH LIBRARY LIVERPOOL L17 6BD
TEL. 0151 231 5216/5299

Dear Parent or Carer

This activity will help your child to realise that we can measure lengths which are not straight lines. Help your child to count the metres and centimetres as accurately as possible.

_____and

child

_____

helper(s)

_____

did this activity together

_____and

child

_____

helper(s)

_____

did this activity together

Jumps

● Stand in one spot and jump forwards as far as possible.

● Ask someone to mark the place where you land.

● Measure your jump in footsteps and write down the answer.

● Do this several times.

I jumped .... footsteps

I jumped .... footsteps

I jumped .... footsteps

I jumped .... footsteps

● What is your longest jump?

● What is your shortest?

Aeroplanes

YOU WILL NEED: some paper; a piece of string 1 metre long; a pencil and a willing partner.

● Make a paper aeroplane:

Fold in half

Fold down one corner

Fold down the other corner

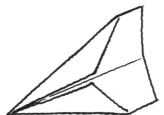

Fold over each side again to make a point.

Fold down the edges to make wings

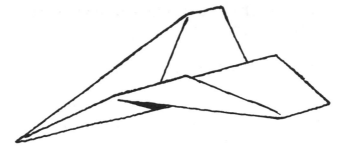

● How far can you make it fly?
(You may need to do this outdoors.)

● Ask your partner to mark where it lands and then use your piece of string to measure the distance it flew.

● Do this several times. Write the distances below.

My plane flew .... cm

My plane flew .... cm

My plane flew .... cm

My plane flew .... cm

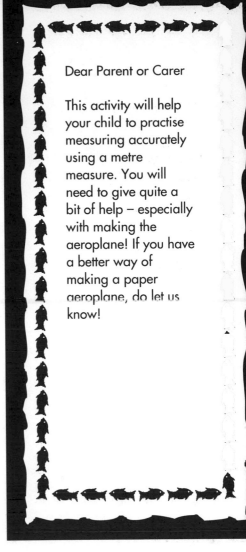

Dear Parent or Carer

This activity will help your child to practise measuring accurately using a metre measure. You will need to give quite a bit of help – especially with making the aeroplane! If you have a better way of making a paper aeroplane, do let us know!

_____and

child

_____

helper(s)

_____

did this activity together

Dear Parent or Carer

This activity will help your child to practise measuring using a metre strip accurately. We shall use all the information from this work back in class.

_____and

child

_____

helper(s)

_____

did this activity together

Armspans and heights

YOU WILL NEED: a pencil; 2 books and some string.

Your armspan – the distance from fingertip to fingertip if you stretch your arms and fingers as wide as you can – is supposed to be the same as your height. Measure your armspan, and that of another person in your family, to see if this is true.

● Lie down on the floor and ask someone to put a book by your head and a book by your feet. Get up slowly, being careful not to disturb the books. Measure the distance between the books carefully. Write down your answer.

My height is .... cm

● Now take your string or wool and ask your partner to stretch it from your fingertip to fingertip when you are holding your arms outstretched. Measure the piece of string and write down your answer.

My armspan is .... cm

● Do this for someone else in your home and write down your findings.

Name: ....

Their height is .... cm

Their armspan is .... cm

impact MATHS HOMEWORK

Body measures

YOU WILL NEED: paper; scissors and a ruler.

● Make a strip of paper the same length as your handspan and cubit. (If you do not know what a cubit is, look it up in the dictionary – the pictures below may help!)

● Estimate how many times your handspan fits into your cubit.

● Check this out by measuring. Were you right?

● Look at the handspan and cubit of a grown-up in your home. Make paper strips to fit them.

● Estimate how many times their handspan fits into their cubit.

● Now check.

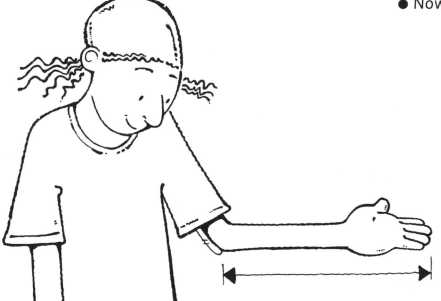

A cubit

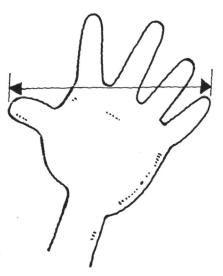

A handspan

impact MATHS HOMEWORK

Dear Parent or Carer

This activity will help your child to compare and estimate accurately. We are going to use the handspans and cubits back in school to do some measuring using standard units.

_____and
child

_____
helper(s)

_____

did this activity together

Dear Parent or Carer

This activity will give practice in measuring accurately and carefully. Because your child will have to measure things other than straight lines, it will be necessary to devise ways of estimating and checking. We shall use the results for work involving standard units (centimetres) in length.

_____and

child

_____

helper(s)

_____

did this activity together

Long numbers

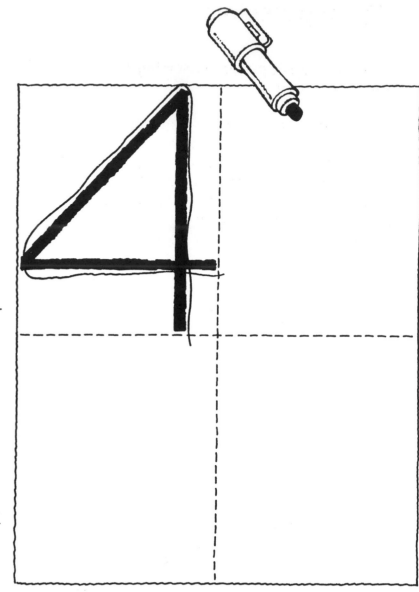

YOU WILL NEED: a piece of paper; a pencil or felt-tipped pen and some string or wool.

● Fold your paper in half lengthways then widthways to make 4 sections.

● Write a number between 2 and 9 (inclusive) in each part. (Use up all the available space in that section for each number.)

● Which numbers do you think will need the longest piece of string to cover them?

● You and your partner each choose 2 of the numbers you have written.

● Now use lengths of your string to check which number is the longest. Lay the string over the pencil/pen line. (Damp string stays in place better.)

● Compare the lengths of string needed for each number.

● Which number is the longest?

impact MATHS HOMEWORK

Diplodocus measures

YOU WILL NEED: a piece of string 1 metre long and a pencil.

A diplodocus was 27 metres long.

● Go somewhere outside – a park, the garden, the street (if it's quiet!) – and use your metre string to work out how far a diplodocus would stretch if he were to walk near your home! (You may need to mark out your measurements in some way.)

● Fill in the answers in the space on the right.

A diplodocus would stretch

from ....

....

to ....

....

● Can you draw a dinosaur?

Dear Parent or Carer

This activity really turns children's attention to larger distances and large numbers of units. Help to work out just how large these creatures were!

_____and
child

_____
helper(s)

did this activity together

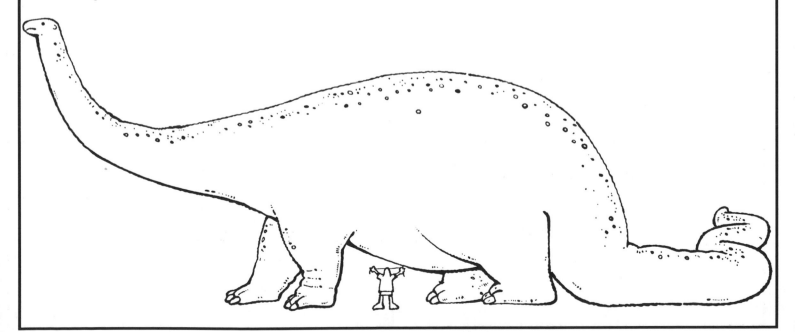

Dear Parent or Carer

This activity will help your child to measure accurately. Fine distinctions between jumps will be needed so perhaps you could discuss half and quarter units – half a decimetre and so on. Encourage your child to be very careful in measuring.

_____and

child

_____

helper(s)

_____

did this activity together

Long jump

YOU WILL NEED: scissors; a pencil and some space to do this activity!

● Ask someone to help you mark a starting place. Jump as far as you can with your feet together and ask your partner to mark where you land.

● Estimate how many decimetres you have jumped. Write down your estimate.

My estimate was .... dm

● Now use the decimetre strip at the bottom of the page to check your estimate. (You will have to cut it out – and it helps if you stick it on a piece of card.) Write down your answer.

My jump was .... dm

● Have 4 or 5 tries. Record your 2 best jumps.

My jump was .... dm

My jump was .... dm

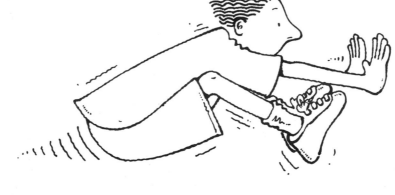

| 0 | 5 | 10 |

Paper chains

YOU WILL NEED: an A4 sheet of paper and some glue, paste, Sellotape, staples or anything else you can think of!

● Make the longest paper chain that you can using an A4 sheet of paper.

You may cut the paper in any way you can think of.

Dear Parent or Carer

This activity draws upon children's mathematical creativity. They will have to consider how best to make a chain – what about the ways in which it is going to hang together? A good ploy is to practise on pieces of newspaper before getting going on the real thing!

_____and

child

_____

helper(s)

_____

did this activity together

Dear Parent or Carer

This activity will help to develop the ability to draw plans – and, in this case, plans to a scale. Your child will need to measure accurately, and will probably require quite a lot of help with thinking through the procedure.

_____and

child

_____

helper(s)

_____

did this activity together

Lengthy plans

YOU WILL NEED: a pencil; squared paper and a piece of string 1 metre long.

● Draw a plan of the room in which your parents cook at home. It should include the windows, the doors and all the furniture.

● You will need to measure the sides of the room with your metre string, and draw them the appropriate length on the squared paper.

● Draw 4 squares for every metre. So if your room is 4 metres long, you will draw the side 16 squares long.

● Draw all the furniture in the same way in the correct place.

impact MATHS HOMEWORK

Timing races

YOU WILL NEED: a piece of string 1 metre in length; a stopwatch or watch with a second hand and a pencil.

How long does it take you to run:

10 metres

25 metres

50 metres

● Ask someone to help you agree a 10m, a 25m and a 50m course which you can run. It could be down your street or across a local park, but you must measure it. Use your metre string to help you.

● Now ask your partner to time you running these races. Write down your times.

10m .... time = ... seconds

25m .... time = ... seconds

50m .... time = ... seconds

Dear Parent or Carer

This activity will help your child to learn to measure quite long distances. These can be very difficult to visualise unless you have actually experienced measuring them yourself.

_____and
child

_____
helper(s)

_____

did this activity together

Dear Parent or Carer

This activity involves a great deal of mathematical thinking and judgement. Your child will need to measure to a fair degree of accuracy. Help as much as you can to achieve this.

_____and

child

_____

helper(s)

_____

did this activity together

Eyesight test

YOU WILL NEED: paper; a pencil; a piece of string 1 metre in length and a ruler.

What is a fair test of your eyesight? With the help of a partner you are going to invent one.

● First of all design an eye-testing board. This will consist of letters or words which start off large and then get smaller and smaller on lines lower down the page. It is important to print these clearly so that no-one will have trouble reading them.

● Now decide what is a reasonable distance to place the board from the person you are testing. Use someone in your house who has quite good eyesight to test it out.

● Measure the distance between them and the board when they can read all the letters or words on the board except the last line. (Use your metre string and a ruler to measure with.)

● Write down the distance in metres and centimetres.

● Over the next few days use your eyesight test on as many people as you can.

● You will have to decide what counts as good eyesight, reasonable eyesight, and poor eyesight!

impact MATHS HOMEWORK

Wrap around

YOU WILL NEED: some circular objects; scissors; paper or string and a pencil.

● Find a circular object, such as a plate, a mat, a wheel, etc.

● Cut a strip of paper or a piece of string the length of the diameter of the object.

● Cut a strip of paper or a piece of string the length of the distance around the object.

● How many times does the first piece of string (the diameter) fit along the second piece of string (the circumference)? Write down your answer.

It fits .... **times**

● Repeat this activity with at least 2 other circular objects.

● What do you notice?

Dear Parent or Carer

This activity leads into a discussion of the relationship between the diameter and the circumference of circles. Your child will need to be fairly accurate when measuring in order to discover this relationship (pi). Please help with the measuring.

_____and

child

_____

helper(s)

_____

did this activity together

impact MATHS HOMEWORK

Dear Parent or Carer

This activity is designed to lead into work exploring the relationship between the circumference (the distance around a circle) and the diameter (the distance across the circle). While engaged in this activity, your child will do a great deal of accurate measuring, in class as well as at home.

_____and

child

_____

helper(s)

_____

did this activity together

Around and about

YOU WILL NEED: string and a pencil.

● You are going to measure the distance around as many things as you can.

● Look around your home and choose something round to measure, such as a plate, a wastepaper basket, a clock, a wheel or anything else you want.

● Think of a way to measure round it accurately. Write your measurement down.

.... **measured**

.... **cm**

● Now measure right across the middle of your object – from edge to edge. Write your measurement down.

.... **measured**

.... **cm**

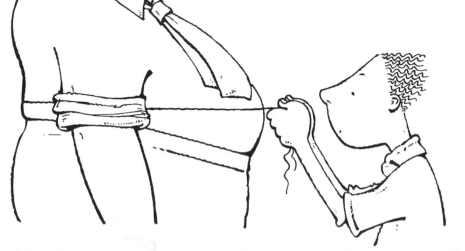

impact MATHS HOMEWORK

Millimetre money

YOU WILL NEED: several coins; a ruler with millimetres on it and a pencil.

● Take it in turns to take a coin.

● First of all, estimate how many millimetres the coin is from edge to edge – going across the middle (the diameter).

● Write down the estimate and the coin you chose in the chart below.

● Now let your partner measure it. Write down the answer. How close were you?

If you were within 3mm above or below the correct amount keep the coin.

● Now let your partner take a different coin and make an estimate. Don't forget to write down your estimates and measurements.

● Keep playing until all the different coins have been chosen. The player with the most money is the winner!

coin	estimate	measurement

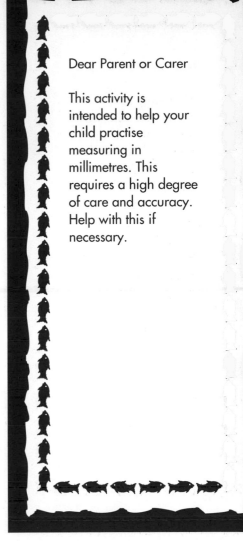

Dear Parent or Carer

This activity is intended to help your child practise measuring in millimetres. This requires a high degree of care and accuracy. Help with this if necessary.

_____and

child

_____

helper(s)

_____

did this activity together

Dear Parent or Carer

This activity asks your child to investigate a hypothesis. The relationship between miles and kilometres is an important one to understand and checking out how to convert quickly and easily will help your child to do this. Please talk about the strategies your child is trying and think things through out loud!

_____and

child

_____

helper(s)

_____

did this activity together

Miles away

In Britain we measure distances in miles. On the Continent, they measure distances in kilometres. It is often confusing – especially if you want to know how far it is to walk or cycle somewhere!

We know that 5 miles is 8 kilometres.

● Can you work out what 10 miles is? Write down your answer.

10 miles = ... km.

What is 15 miles? .... km

What is 20 miles? .... km

● To go from miles to kilometres we multiply by 8 and divide by 5.

● It is said that a quicker way of doing this is to use the Fibonacci sequence, where each number is the sum of the preceding 2 numbers. For example:

1, 1, 2, 3, 5, 8, 13, 21, 34, 55, 89, 144, 233...

So 5 miles is 8km, 13 miles is 21km ...

● Does this always work?

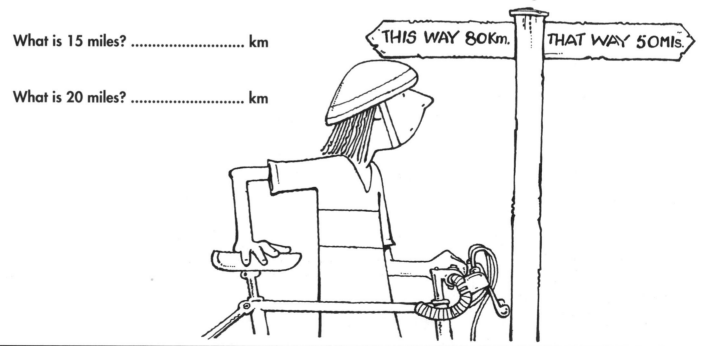

impact MATHS HOMEWORK

Car lengths

If a person wants to take a car on a ferry, they have to declare its length. How long are cars? What is a good unit to use to measure this?

● Find a car that someone will let you measure.

● Estimate its length in metres and centimetres. Write down the type of car and your estimate on a piece of paper.

● Now measure it. What is its actual measurement? Write it down.

● How close were you?

● Let someone else have a guess. Don't show them the actual measurement until they've guessed!

● Collect as many different estimates as you can.

I.M. MARSH LIBRARY LIVERPOOL L17 6BD
TEL. 0151 231 5216/5299

impact MATHS HOMEWORK

Dear Parent or Carer

This activity will help to estimate and measure the length of fairly large objects. Help your child to collect as many other estimates as they can. It is surprising how many adults find it hard to estimate.

_____and

child

_____

helper(s)

_____

did this activity together

Measuring   35

_____and

child

_____

helper(s)

_____

did this activity together

String cuts

YOU WILL NEED: scissors; a ball of string or wool and a ruler with centimetres and millimetres on it.

● Start off by saying a length to your partner. For example: **23cm**.

● They must then attempt to cut a piece of string exactly this long.

● You then measure their piece of string and if they are within 1cm, they can keep it.

If not, they specify a length shorter than the first, and you have to try to cut the piece to make it the length specified. For example: **19cm**.

If you are within 1cm you can keep the string. If not, they then say a length which is even shorter, and continue playing.

If you keep a piece of string, then they must cut the next piece you specify from the ball.

● Keep playing until one of you has 4 pieces. That person is the winner!

impact MATHS HOMEWORK

Thick pages

YOU WILL NEED: a book; a ruler with millimetres (mm) on it and a calculator.

You are going to calculate the thickness of 1 page of a book!

How will you do this?

● Look at your book.

● Talk to your partner about how you intend to do this.

● Now try it out and write down exactly what you have done. Write down your answer.

The thickness of 1 page is .... mm

Dear Parent or Carer

This activity is geared to help children understand and become used to handling very small units, i.e. fractions of a millimetre. The more they have to deal with such units, the happier they feel with them.

_____and

child

_____

helper(s)

_____

did this activity together

Take away

YOU WILL NEED: a dice; a ruler and a pencil and paper.

The pirates are about to make you walk the plank! But before you fall in the sea, you make a plea for mercy and they agree to give you a chance to get back from where you stand, which is 2 metres and 66 centimetres away from both the ends. However, a sea monster is slowly chewing away the end of the plank. Will you survive until he reaches your starting position?

● Throw the dice twice. Make a 2-figure number from the numbers thrown, for example 63 or 36. This is the number of centimetres you may move back. (You will need to mark out your moves on paper.)

● Now let your partner have a turn. They throw the dice and make a 2-figure number, for example 34 or 43. This is the number of centimetres the monster bites off the plank.

● Keep playing and mark off the length of the plank and your position on it each turn. Do you move back to the end before the monster eats your plank?

NB: If the monster eats to the centre (2m 66cm) before you reach the ship then life becomes very dangerous!

impact MATHS HOMEWORK

Cassette lengths

How long – in metres and centimetres –
is the average cassette tape?

Without breaking one, can you make a
sensible estimate and check it out?

● Think about ways of working this out
and discuss them with your partner.

● When you have found a way, write it
down next to your answer.

Dear Parent or Carer

This activity is meant
to stimulate creative
mathematical thinking
in terms of solving a
problem and
measuring a 'curled
up' length with
standard units. The
best way to help is to
talk about it – puzzle
over it – with your
child.

_____and

child

_____

helper(s)

_____

did this activity together

LIVERPOOL JOHN MOORES UNIVERSITY
LEARNING SERVICES

Dear Parent or Carer

This activity takes patience and perseverance. Your child will be adding up measurements, converting from metres to kilometres and also making a series of estimates. These all involve complex mathematical thinking.

_____and

child

_____

helper(s)

_____

did this activity together

Walk about

How far do you walk in an ordinary day?

How will you make a sensible estimate of this?

● Begin by charting your movements – out of your bedroom, to the bathroom …

● Count it up in metres and then – as you leave the house and walk longer distances – in kilometres. Make as careful and complete a chart as you can.

● Can you make a good estimate of how far you walk on a typical school day? Write down your answer.

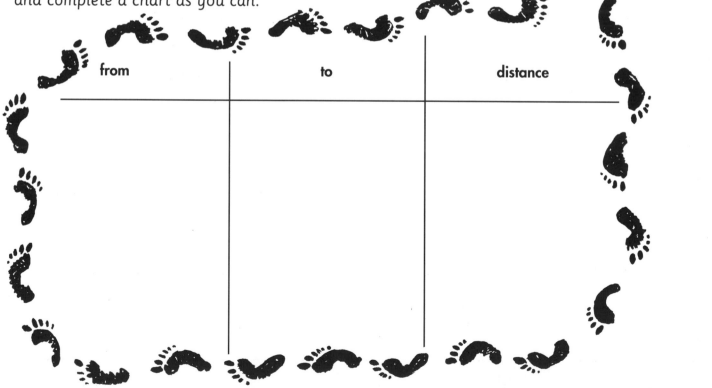

from	to	distance

Faster, faster

YOU WILL NEED: a stopwatch or watch with a second hand; a piece of string 1 metre in length and a pencil.

How fast can you crawl?

How fast can you hop?

To do this you will need to time yourself.

● Decide what distance you are going to crawl. Map out a course! Make it an exact number of metres, for example 10 metres, or more if possible.

● Now ask your partner to time you – they will need a watch with seconds on it.

READY, STEADY, GO!

● Write down how long it took you.

● Write down the distance you crawled.

● Now divide the first figure by the second figure. This is your speed in metres per second. Write down your answer.

● Repeat this for hopping (1 leg only!) if you can!

● Which was faster?

time	distance	speed

Dear Parent or Carer

This activity introduces the idea that we can measure our speed of movement. We are encouraging the children to talk about fast and slow and what these terms mean. Help your child to design a course and to measure the speed.

_____and

child

_____

helper(s)

_____

did this activity together

Speed signs

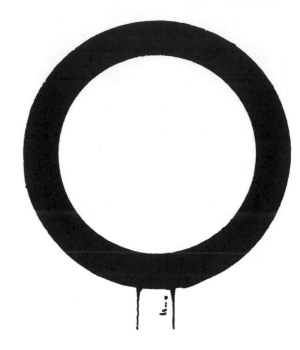

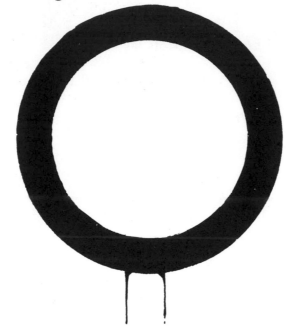

Speed signs are those which tell you how fast you are allowed to drive (or cycle!).

For example, you often see a 30mph sign as you enter a built-up area.

● Look out for as many different examples of speed signs as you can. Draw them on a piece of paper. They are often small and on lampposts, at the entrances to side roads or can be seen on a car or bus journey.

● Which is the lowest speed? Write your answer on the sign on the left.

● Which is the highest? Write the answer on the sign on the right.

● What do the speed signs look like in other countries, such as France, Germany or the USA?

REMEMBER: Be careful of moving vehicles when looking at road signs.

_____and

child

_____

helper(s)

_____

did this activity together

impact MATHS HOMEWORK

Tin areas

YOU WILL NEED: a tin; a pencil and squared paper.

You are going to design a label for a tin. It can be a tin of any food you like! First you need to make a label of the right size.

● Borrow a tin from the cupboard and draw a straight line down the label.

● Put the tin on its side and carefully place the line along one edge of the squared paper.

● Now carefully roll the tin in 1 complete circle so that the line you draw is just visible again.

● Draw another line down the squared paper at this point. Mark the top and the bottom of the tin and draw two straight lines horizontally. This is the size of your label.

● Work out its area in squares and write down the answer.

My label is .... squares

● Now make a design for your label.

Dear Parent or Carer

Encourage your child to be systematic about counting the squares. They might like to estimate first, count then check the answer on the calculator.

_____and

child

_____

helper(s)

_____

did this activity together

_____and

child

_____

helper(s)

_____

did this activity together

Box areas

YOU WILL NEED: a small box; squared paper and a pencil.

You are going to measure the area of a box.

● First of all, find a small box.

● Draw round each of its faces on the squared paper using a different colour for each face. Make sure you draw every face!

● Count up the number of squares on each face and write it down.

● Add up the numbers. What is the total area of the box?

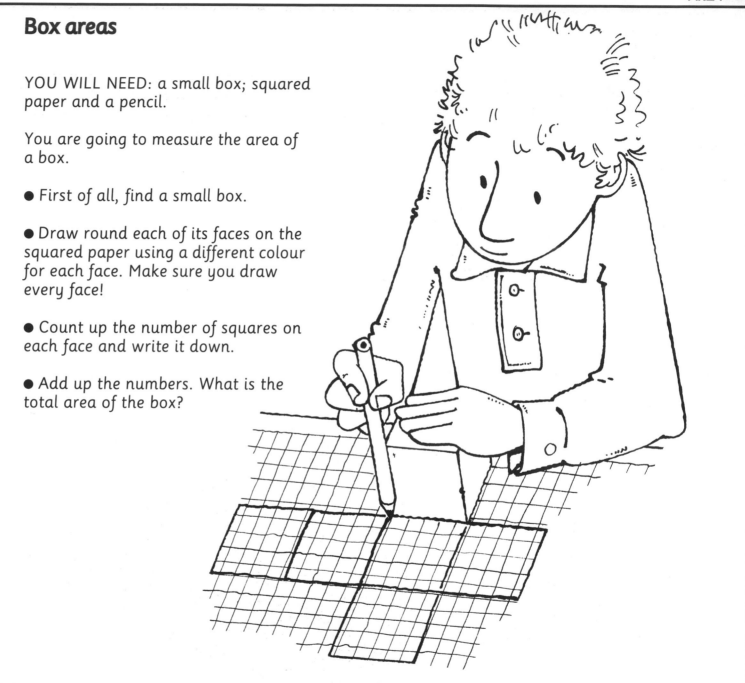

impact MATHS HOMEWORK

Metre of fun

YOU WILL NEED: string; scissors; toys, comics, books and a pencil.

● Cut 4 pieces of string, each 1 metre long.

● Use your metre strings to mark out an area of 1 square metre on the floor of your home.

● How many toys can you fit on your square metre of floor? Fit as many toys on it as you can. If you run out of toys – how about books and comics?

● Make a list of all the things that you managed to fit on to your square metre.

my list of toys

Dear Parent or Carer

Help your child to make a square metre out of newspaper. Objects could be placed on the newspaper and drawn round to find the best arrangement.

_____and

child

_____

helper(s)

_____

did this activity together

impact MATHS HOMEWORK

Dear Parent or Carer

It will be useful if you demonstrate to your child how multiplication can be used to find the area of squares and rectangles.

_____and

child

_____

helper(s)

_____

did this activity together

Window panes

What is the area of the window in the room where you sleep?

You can calculate this fairly easily.

● Draw a picture of the window – draw only 1 pane if it has more than 1 pane of glass.

● Use the decimetre strip at the bottom of this page to measure the longer edge of the window. Write the number on the long edge of your drawing.

● Now measure the shorter edge of the window and write the number on the short edge of your drawing.

● Multiply these 2 numbers to find the area of the pane. Use a calculator to help you do this if you need to. Write the answer next to your drawing.

● How many panes are there in your window?

0   5   10

impact MATHS HOMEWORK

Jigsaw areas

YOU WILL NEED:
scissors; some crayons or
felt-tipped pens and
someone to help you.

● You are going to make
a jigsaw using the
square on the right.

● Colour the square as
follows:

Colour A – one quarter of
the total area (36
squares)

Colour B – one quarter of
the total area (36
squares)

Colour C – one third of
the total area (48
squares)

Colour D – one sixth
of the total area (24
squares)

● Now cut it up into
small squares. Can you
put it back together?

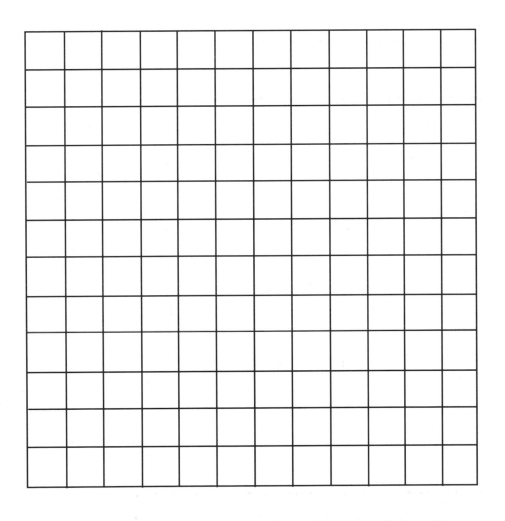

Dear Parent or Carer

Allow your child time
to investigate this
activity. Try folding the
square or calculate
using paper and
pencil or a calculator
to find the answers.

_____and

child

_____

helper(s)

_____

did this activity together

impact MATHS HOMEWORK

_____and

child

_____

helper(s)

_____

did this activity together

Decimetre boxes

YOU WILL NEED: scissors;
glue; crayons and a pencil.

● Make a box using the net on
this page.

● First cut it out and decorate
the faces then fold them to
make a box. Use the tabs to
stick it together.

● What is the area of each face
of your box? Write down your
answers.

**Each face is .... square
centimetres.**

● What is its surface area?

**The surface area is .... square
centimetres.**

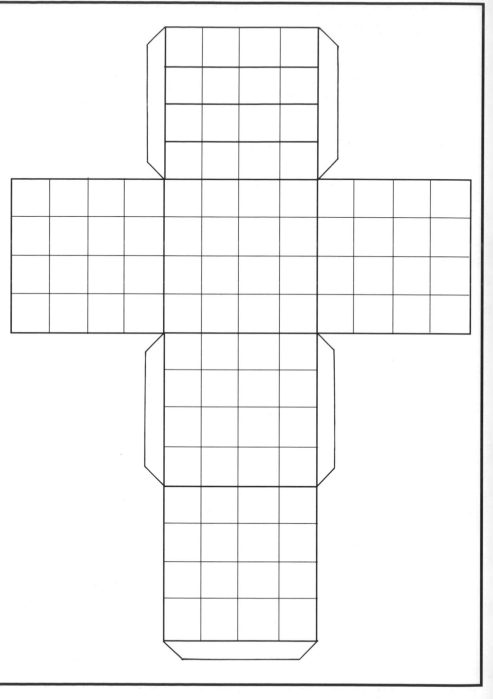

impact MATHS HOMEWORK

Letter areas

● Draw your initials on the dotted area below.

● Write the letters by joining dots. Make them as large as you can.
(An example is given for you.)

● Colour them in.

● Work out their area and their perimeter. Write down your answers.

The perimeter is the distance around the letter.

The area is the number of squares it covers.

Dear Parent or Carer

Encourage your child to estimate the perimeters and areas before counting.

_____and

child

_____

helper(s)

_____

did this activity together

Toy areas

YOU WILL NEED: a small toy; squared paper and a pencil.

● Choose a small fairly flat toy that will fit on to the squared paper.

● Lay it flat and draw round it.

● Colour it in.

● Now work out its area in squares. Write down your answer.

The area is .... squares

_____and

child

_____

helper(s)

_____

did this activity together

impact MATHS HOMEWORK

Handy area

YOU WILL NEED: squared paper; crayons and a pencil.

● Draw round your hand on the squared paper. (Keep your fingers together – it's easier!)

● How many squares does your hand cover? Colour it in and count as you colour. Write down your answer.

The area of my hand is .... squares

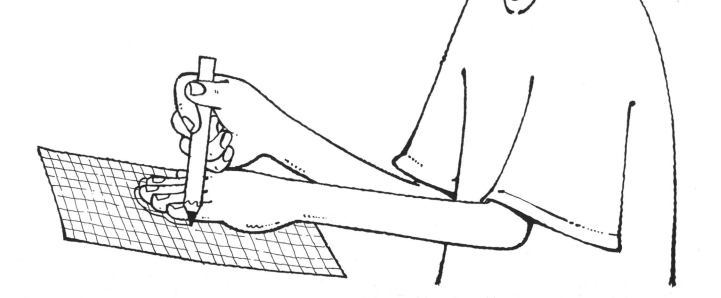

Dear Parent or Carer

Encourage your child to be systematic about counting the squares.

_____and

child

_____

helper(s)

_____

did this activity together

Dear Parent or Carer

Your child may like to cut out several decimetre squares and arrange them on to a piece of paper the same size as your TV screen. Once the best arrangements have been found you could stick them down and count them.

The big screen

YOU WILL NEED: the decimetre square from the bottom of this page, mounted on card and a TV screen to measure.

● How many of the squares do you think will cover the TV screen? Write down your estimate.

My estimate: ....

● Ask your partner to estimate as well. Write down their answer.

My partner's estimate: ....

● Now use your square to measure it accurately. Don't forget to count half squares. Write down the answer.

The TV screen was .... squares in area

● Draw a TV screen with a picture of your favourite programme on it!

_____and

child

_____

helper(s)

_____

did this activity together

Perimeters

YOU WILL NEED: squared paper and a pencil.

These oblongs have the same area but the distance around them (the perimeter) is different.

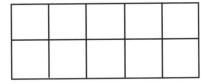

● Draw 4 different rectangles all with an area of 24 squares on the sheet of squared paper. What are their perimeters?

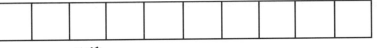

● Draw 4 different rectangles all with a perimeter of 36 units. What are their areas?

Dear Parent or Carer

This activity explores the difference between the area of a shape and the distance round it. These are mathematical concepts which children need to grasp well. Please discuss this with your child.

_____and

child

_____

helper(s)

_____

did this activity together

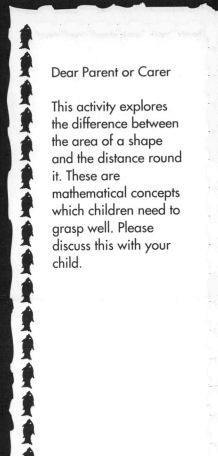

impact MATHS HOMEWORK

Dear Parent or Carer

This activity will help your child to see how, if the length of a side is doubled, the area of the shape is quadrupled! The ideas and measurements involved in enlargements are complex. Please discuss this activity with your child.

_____and

child

_____

helper(s)

_____

did this activity together

Enlarging a picture

YOU WILL NEED: a pencil and crayons.

● Draw a simple picture on the small grid below. It should be simple – an outline only!

● Now use the larger grid and draw your picture again, putting exactly the same parts in each quadrant.

● Colour in both pictures.

● How much larger is the area of your second picture?

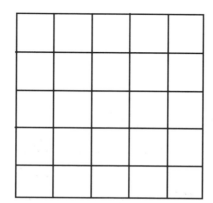

impact MATHS HOMEWORK

Boxing clever

YOU WILL NEED: squared paper;
a pencil and scissors.

● Make a box with a surface area of 88 square centimetres.

● Ask your partner to help you work out the dimensions of your box. Remember the total surface area must be 88 squares.

There is more than one way of doing this!

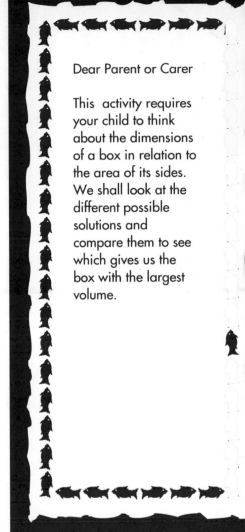

Dear Parent or Carer

This activity requires your child to think about the dimensions of a box in relation to the area of its sides. We shall look at the different possible solutions and compare them to see which gives us the box with the largest volume.

_____and

child

_____

helper(s)

_____

did this activity together

Surfaces

It is difficult to judge the surface area of an object. Sometimes when you need to paint it or sand it or wash it you realise that it has a much larger surface area than you had thought.

● Does your arm have a larger surface area than a TV screen?

● How will you find out?

● Write down the answer and your way of finding out.

HINT:
Newspaper could be useful!

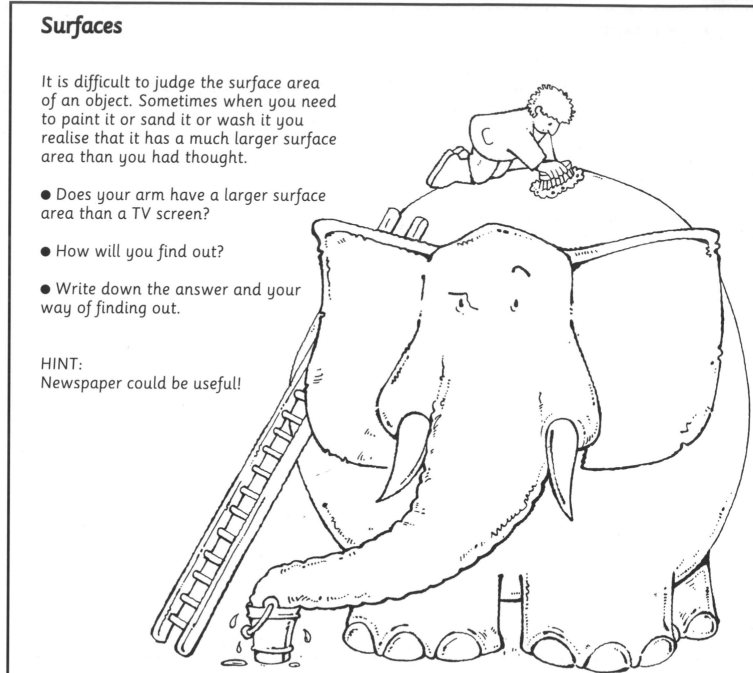

impact MATHS HOMEWORK

Circular hunt

YOU WILL NEED: some small circular objects; squared paper and a pencil.

● Look around your house to find 3 or 4 circular things which all fit on to the squared paper.

● Draw carefully around each one, starting with the smallest.

● Each time draw in the radius (the distance from the centre to the edge of the circle).

● Measure the radius.

● Count the squares to find the area of each circle.

● Write down your findings in the chart below.

object	radius	area

Dear Parent or Carer

We are working on the relationship between the area of a circle and its radius. Clearly this will lead to work on *pi*, but in this activity we are not yet using this ratio. Help your child to find circles and to draw carefully and obtain accurate measurements.

_____and

child

_____

helper(s)

_____

did this activity together

Secret garden

YOU WILL NEED: squared paper and a pencil.

A friend has a garden that is 84 square metres in area.

She has asked you to buy fencing for her garden but she has not told you the shape or the length of the perimeter.

● What is the shortest length of fence she would need? What shape would her garden be in this case?

● What is the longest length of fencing? What shape would it be in this case?

● Use squared paper to help you work this out.

impact MATHS HOMEWORK

Handful of water

YOU WILL NEED: a medicine spoon – or, if you haven't got one, a teaspoon; a small bowl and somewhere to work where you can safely tip water!

How much water can you hold in your hands?

Do this experiment to find out.

● Fill your hands with water. Hold them like a cup to hold as much water as you can.

● Tip the water into the bowl.

● Now count how many spoonfuls of water there are in the bowl. Write down your answer.

My handful of water was .... spoonfuls

Dear Parent or Carer

You could extend this activity by including other members of the family. Record the number of spoonfuls that each family member can hold in their cupped hands.

_____and
child

_____
helper(s)

_____
did this activity together

I.M. MARSH LIBRARY LIVERPOOL L17 6BD
TEL. 0151 231 5216/5299

impact MATHS HOMEWORK

Measuring 59

Dear Parent or Carer

Estimating capacity is very difficult! Your child may like to estimate smaller containers first, for example bowls or buckets.

_____and

child

_____

helper(s)

_____

did this activity together

Bath count up

How much water is there in a bath?

● First you need to decide on a good unit to use to measure it. You could use a litre ... or a pint ... or another unit.

● When you next have a bath, ask someone to help you estimate and then check how much water there is in the bath. Write down your answers.

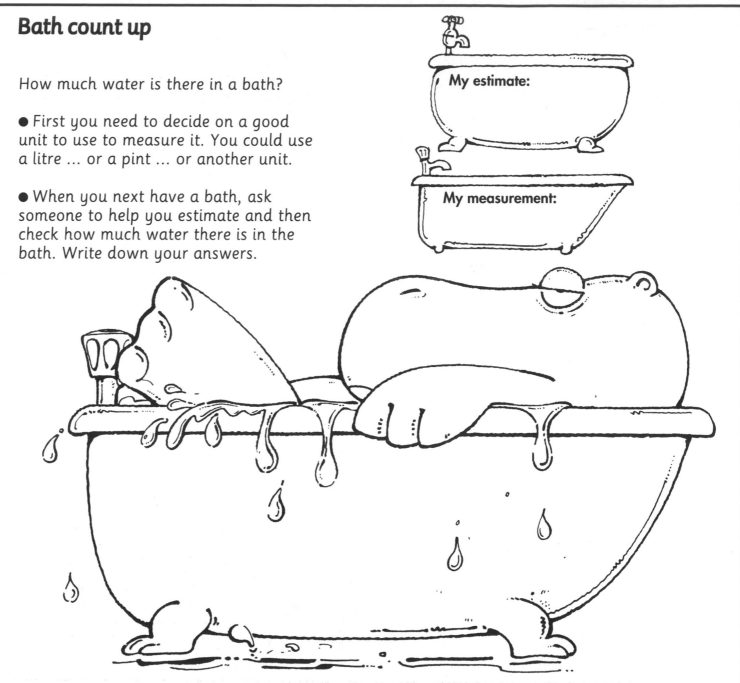

My estimate:

My measurement:

impact MATHS HOMEWORK

Guess along

YOU WILL NEED: some different-sized containers – all about cup/mug size; a medicine spoon (a teaspoon will do if you can't find one) and a place to do the activity – where it does not matter if you make a mess!

How good are you at guessing how much a cup, mug, beaker, glass or anything else holds?

● Choose a mug then both you and your partner estimate how many spoonfuls it will hold. Write down your estimates.

● Now measure to see who was right. You can use water, or lentils, or rice, or salt, or even sugar!

● The person who was nearest keeps the mug.

● Now choose a different cup and both estimate again. Write down your estimates. Again the person who is nearest takes the cup.

● Keep playing until you have tested all the cups/mugs/glasses. Who has the most?

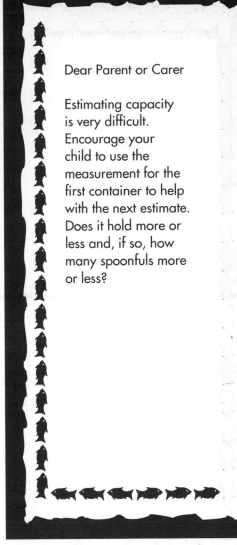

Dear Parent or Carer

Estimating capacity is very difficult. Encourage your child to use the measurement for the first container to help with the next estimate. Does it hold more or less and, if so, how many spoonfuls more or less?

_____and

child

_____

helper(s)

_____

did this activity together

Dear Parent or Carer

If your child is using a medicine spoon (capacity 5ml), counting in fives could be encouraged. Is there anything at home that has the same capacity or similar capacity to your estimate, such as a shampoo bottle?

_____and

child

_____

helper(s)

_____

did this activity together

100ml and counting

YOU WILL NEED: a medicine spoon (a teaspoon will do if you can't find one!); a small cup; some lentils or rice or salt and a dice.

● Throw the dice twice and add the totals together. Count that many spoonfuls of rice, and put them in the cup. Write down the number of spoonfuls you take in the table below.

● Now let your partner take a turn.

● Keep taking it in turns to throw the dice. Don't forget to write down the number of spoonfuls each time.

● When the cup overflows stop playing!

● Add up the number of spoonfuls you each took. The player with the most is the winner!

player 1	player 2

impact MATHS HOMEWORK

Bathroom lookout

● Look in your bathroom. How many containers can you see?

● Look at the units their contents are measured in. How many are less than 1 litre? Write their names in the chart.

● How many are less than half a litre? Write down their names below.

● How many are less than a quarter of a litre? Write down their names below.

REMEMBER: 1 litre   = 1000ml
                        = 1000cc

● Draw the containers on another piece of paper or the back of this sheet.

less than 1 litre	less than half a litre	less than quarter of a litre

Dear Parent or Carer

Help your child to be systematic when sorting the containers. Remember that half a litre is 500ml and a quarter is 250ml.

_____and

child

_____

helper(s)

_____

did this activity together

Dear Parent or Carer

Encourage your child to look at litre measurements on a variety of containers in supermarkets and at home.

_____and

child

_____

helper(s)

_____

did this activity together

Make a litre

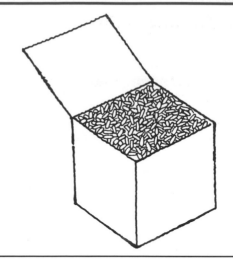

YOU WILL NEED: scissors; glue and some lentils or rice or sugar or salt.

You are going to make a cube that holds exactly 1 litre!

● Draw round the decimetre square 5 times to make a shape like this:

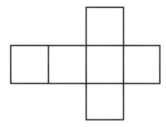

● Now add some tabs (pieces that you can use to stick the sides together) to the edge of the squares.

● Finally, cut it all out, fold it up and stick it together to make a litre cube. (Leave one side open to make a lid.)

● Test it out. Find a litre container, fill it with lentils or rice or sugar or salt... then tip the contents into the cube. Does it fit?

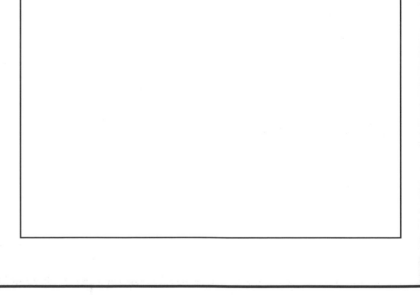

impact MATHS HOMEWORK

How much do they hold?

YOU WILL NEED: a sheet of paper; cornflakes and a pencil.

You can make 2 different cylinders using this sheet of A4 paper.

A tall thin one can be made by rolling it lengthways!

A short fat one can be made by rolling it widthways!

● Which one holds the most – or do they hold the same?

● Ask as many people as you can to guess first. Make a list of their guesses.

● Now test it out. Fill the long thin one with cornflakes. Tip it out on to a piece of paper, keeping the cornflakes together.

● Make the short fat cylinder. Tip the cornflakes on the paper into this cylinder.

● What do you find out?

● Who was right?

name	guess

Dear Parent or Carer

Be careful, when making the cylinder, that you stick the edges together without overlapping the paper.

_____and

child

_____

helper(s)

_____

did this activity together

Dear Parent or Carer

Your child may like to look at containers which are measured in millilitres. It would be useful to try to estimate the volume of the tin before measuring.

_____and

child

_____

helper(s)

_____

did this activity together

Tin volumes

YOU WILL NEED: an empty tin can; water; a medicine spoon or teaspoon and a pencil.

How much does an ordinary tin can hold? You are going to measure how much a tin holds in millilitres (ml). A medicine spoon – or a teaspoon – is 5ml.

Does it depend on what is in it?

● Ask someone if they will help you.

● Find an empty tin. (BE CAREFUL of any sharp edges.)

● With the help of your partner, count how many medicine spoons of water you can fit into an empty tin. Write down your answer.

My tin held .... spoonfuls

● Now work out how many millilitres your tin holds if each spoon holds 5ml. Write down your answer.

My tin holds .... ml

impact MATHS HOMEWORK

Litres and pints

YOU WILL NEED: a large bowl; a milk bottle/carton that holds 1 pint; a fruit juice bottle/carton that holds 1 litre; water and a pencil.

Some people prefer to measure things in pints. Others prefer to measure in litres!

We are going to work out what the relationship is between pints and litres.

● Find a large bowl, an empty milk bottle or carton (1 pint) and an empty juice carton (1 litre).

● Fill the bowl using the litre carton. How many cartonfuls did it take? Write down your answer.

● Fill the bowl using the pint container. How many did it take? Write down your answer.

It took   It took

_____ pints   _____ litres

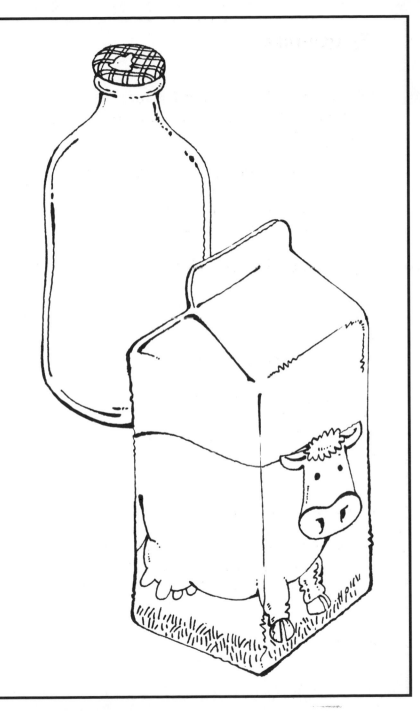

Dear Parent or Carer

Your child may like to investigate the relationship between pints and litres.

_____and

child

_____

helper(s)

_____

did this activity together

I.M. MARSH LIBRARY LIVERPOOL L17 6BD
TEL. 0151 231 5216/5299

Dear Parent or Carer

It will be useful if you help your child to make a decimetre cube. This will assist in the calculation of the volume of the drawer.

_____and

child

_____

helper(s)

_____

did this activity together

Drawer measures

You are going to measure the volume of a drawer.

● Choose a drawer. Draw a sketch of it on a piece of paper.

● Cut out the decimetre strip below and use it to measure its length. Write the measurement on the sketch.

● Use the decimetre strip to measure its width. Write the measurement on the sketch.

● Use the decimetre strip to measure its depth. Write the measurement on the sketch.

To work out the volume: Multiply the number of decimetres along the length by the number along the width. This tells us how many decimetres fit on to the bottom of the drawer. Then multiply the answer by the number of decimetres that fit along the depth. This tells us how many layers there are piled up in the drawer (the volume).

The volume of my drawer is ....

You may need a calculator to help you multiply.

A cubic decimetre is a litre! So the number of cubic decimetres is the number of litres.

You have now found the volume of your drawer in litres!

0   5   10

impact MATHS HOMEWORK

Largest cube

● Make the largest cube possible from an A4 sheet of paper. (You could use this sheet if you wish.)

Dear Parent or Carer

This activity is investigational in nature. It sets up a practical mathematical problem and does not attempt to tell children how to solve it. They have to find their own strategies. It is important that children do sometimes have to think out their own way of solving something rather than simply following a method they have been given.

_____and

child

_____

helper(s)

_____

did this activity together

Dear Parent or Carer

This activity involves some quite hard mathematical thinking. Developing strategic and logical thought is important at this stage of children's development. Help your child by talking through the problem.

_____and

child

_____

helper(s)

_____

did this activity together

Boxes of rice

YOU WILL NEED: card; a pair of kitchen scales; a packet of rice (or sugar or salt); a patient helper and somewhere it does not matter if you make a mess!

● Weigh out 250g of rice.

● Use some card to make a box which will hold this exact amount of rice. You do not need to make a lid.

● Weigh out 500g of rice.

● Make a second box which will hold this exact amount of rice. Again, with no lid.

● How much bigger are the edges on the second box? Are they twice as long? If not, why not?

This diagram shows how you can make a box. If you cut out the shape, fold along the dotted lines and stick the edges together you have made a box.

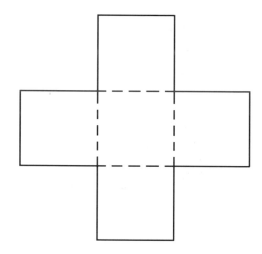

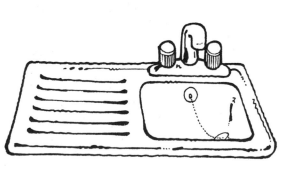

impact MATHS HOMEWORK

Brick pretence

You have been given a brick!

It is a magic brick made up of lots of little bricks.

There are 10 rows of 8 on the bottom layer, and there are 6 layers.

The magician who gave you the brick says that 'If you dip the brick in water, all the small bricks which get 1 wet face will turn into silver! All the small bricks which get 2 wet faces will turn into gold! And all the small bricks which get 3 wet faces will turn into chocolate!'

● How many silver, gold and chocolate bricks will you have? Write down your answers.

● Is it possible to stick all the small bricks together to make a different shaped brick which will give you more gold, silver and chocolate?

Dear Parent or Carer

This activity is great fun if you approach it together. Everyone will have their opinion as to how many of the blocks are in which position! It is important to let your child give reasons for the answers. It may help to draw or make a model of the brick.

_____and

child

_____

helper(s)

_____

did this activity together

Dear Parent or Carer

This activity demonstrates the difference between the capacity and the volume of an object. In this case (unusually!) the capacity is larger than the volume! Encourage your child to be as accurate as possible.

_____and

child

_____

helper(s)

_____

did this activity together

Balloon difference

YOU WILL NEED: a balloon, a cup, a saucer and a 5ml spoon.

You are going to find the volume of the balloon, its capacity and the difference between the two.

The volume is the amount of space the object takes up.

The capacity is the amount it will contain.

● First of all blow up your balloon a few times and let it down again.

● Then find a cup and a small bowl. Fill the cup with water and stand it in the bowl. Make sure that the water is right up to the top.

● Very gently immerse the balloon (not blown up) in the cup, allowing some water to spill over into the bowl.

● Remove the balloon then gently lift the cup out of the bowl and measure the water in the bowl using a 5ml medicine spoon. How many millilitres are there? This is the volume of the balloon.

● Now measure the capacity of the balloon by filling it to the brim with water.

● Tip the water into the bowl and measure how much there is using the 5ml medicine spoon. This is the capacity of the balloon. Write down your answer.

● Which is larger, the balloon's capacity or its volume? What is the difference?

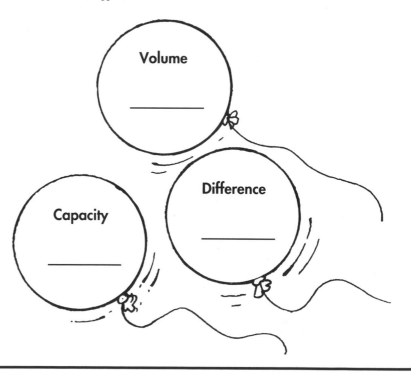

impact MATHS HOMEWORK

Calculate or measure

YOU WILL NEED: a small box; a ruler; a 5ml teaspoon; a small cup; some rice, lentils or sugar; a washable felt-tipped pen and a calculator.

● First of all, create a 100 millilitre measure by counting 20 spoonfuls of rice (20 x 5 = 100) into the small cup. Make a mark with the felt-tipped pen so that you remember the level. You can now use this to measure 100ml.

● Now measure the number of millilitres that your box holds. Do this by counting 100ml at a time into it,

until it is nearly full) then use the teaspoon and count in fives. Write down your answer.

● Now measure the length, width and depth of the box using a centimetre ruler.

● Write down these measures and use your calculator to multiply them together. This is another way of finding the volume. Write down your answer.

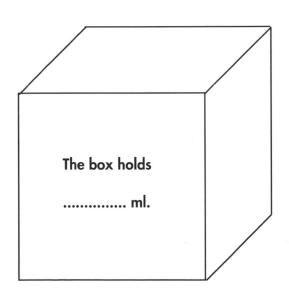

The box holds

.... **ml.**

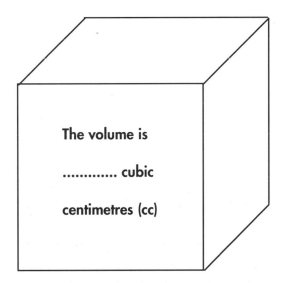

The volume is

.... **cubic**

centimetres (cc)

● How do the 2 figures compare? (1cc = 1ml so they should be about the same!)

Dear Parent or Carer

This activity is quite demanding and you will probably need to give quite a bit of support. Encourage your child to measure as accurately as possible – and to take care with all the different stages. Talking through the activity with your child is probably the best way to help understand it.

_____and

child

_____

helper(s)

_____

did this activity together

_____and

child

_____

helper(s)

_____

did this activity together

Pet weights

YOU WILL NEED: to 'borrow' a pet for a short while!

You are going to judge the weight of a pet – it could be a dog, a cat, a guinea-pig, a rabbit – or anything you like (providing you have ASKED the owner and it is SAFE!).

● Lift the pet gently.

● Try to judge how many kilograms it weighs. Write down your estimate.

● Now can you find a way of weighing the pet?

You could stand on the bathroom scales yourself, ask someone to read how much you weigh, then stand on the scales holding the pet and see how much more you are! You could put the pet on the scales, or on the kitchen scales if it is small enough. You could look in a book about that type of animal and see if it gives average weights. You could try asking the owner!

● Write down the real weight then draw the pet on a piece of paper.

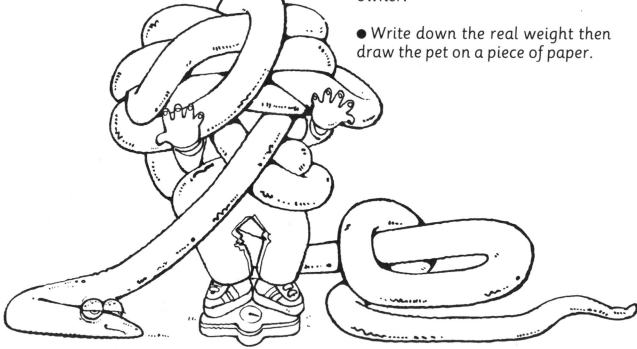

impact MATHS HOMEWORK

Weighing ten

YOU WILL NEED: kitchen scales or balances; 10 fairly small objects, and a pencil.

You are going to weigh 1 object and write down its weight in grams. It could be edible – like an apple, or a potato, or a small packet of raisins. It could be non-edible like a shoe or a book. Write down the name of the object and its weight.

The object I have chosen to weigh is

....

It weighs .... grams

● Now work out how many grams you think 10 of these will weigh. Write down your estimate.

My estimate is .... grams

● Now weigh 10 of them. Were you right? What did they weigh? Write down your answer.

My 10 objects weighed .... grams

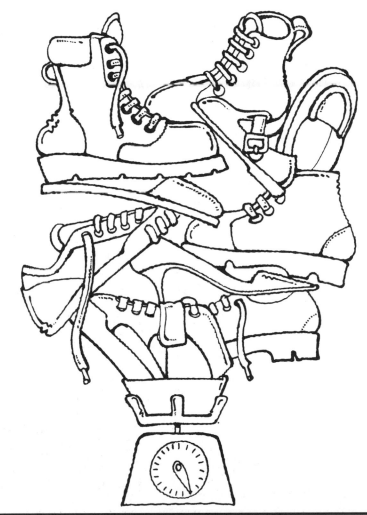

Dear Parent or Carer

Try to encourage your child to be methodical when weighing the articles. If you only have one item you will need to calculate the answer either with paper and pencil or a calculator.

_____and

child

_____

helper(s)

_____

did this activity together

LIVERPOOL JOHN MOORES UNIVERSITY
LEARNING SERVICES

Dear Parent or Carer

Encourage your child
to weigh other objects.
It is often surprising to
discover that a kilo
can look very different
depending on the item
being weighed.

_____and

child

_____

helper(s)

_____

did this activity together

Race to one kilo

YOU WILL NEED: some scales or a
balance that can weigh 1 kilogram
(you could always make a balance using
a coat-hanger and a packet of sugar
(1kg); something that you can spoon and
weigh, like rice or lentils or sugar;
a tablespoon and a dice.

● Take it in turns to throw the dice
twice. Add the totals, and collect that
number of spoonfuls of rice.

● Place the rice on the scales.

● Keep playing until one person puts
on the spoonful which pushes the
weight over 1 kilogram. That person
is the winner!

● Can you predict which
spoonful is going to do this?

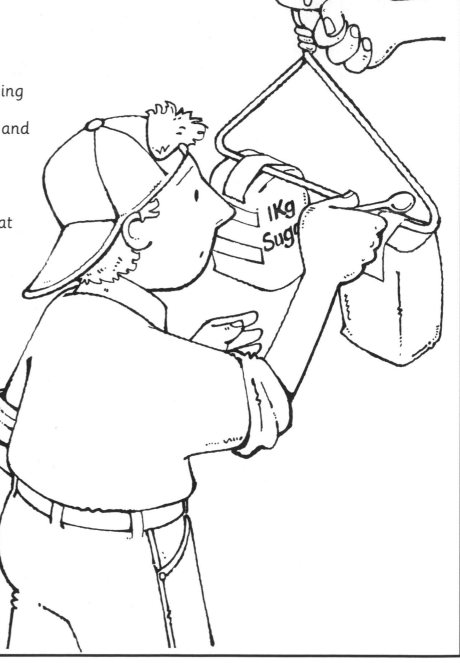

impact MATHS HOMEWORK

Make your own weights

YOU WILL NEED: a balance or kitchen scales.

You are going to invent your own set of weights. You will need a set which will enable you to weigh something to the nearest 100 grams and up to 1kg.

● Which weights will you need?

   A 100 gram weight
   A 200 gram weight

   and which others?

● Find objects – toys, old batteries, pebbles, even a book (!) – which weigh exactly the weights you have decided you need.

● You will have to check that they do weigh what you want them to. For example, your 500 gram weight must actually weigh 500 grams!

● If possible bring all your weights into school.

Dear Parent or Carer

You may need to stick objects together or fill containers with loose items to make the exact weights.

_____and

child

_____

helper(s)

_____

did this activity together

Weigh a handful

YOU WILL NEED: cornflakes, rice or sugar; a balance or some scales and a pencil.

How much does a handful of rice or sugar or cornflakes or anything else weigh?

● Choose a substance that you can hold in your hand. Write down its name in the chart below.

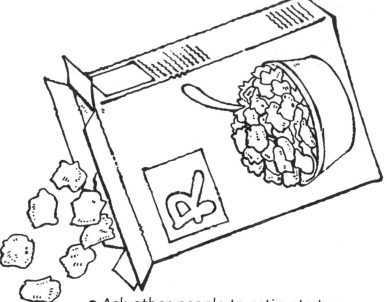

● Estimate how much you think a handful will weigh.

● Ask other people to estimate too. Record the estimates in the chart.

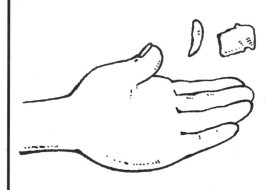

Person's name	Their guess
Substance:	**Actual weight:**

● Now weigh your handful!

● Who was nearest?

_____ and

child

_____

helper(s)

_____

did this activity together

impact MATHS HOMEWORK

Cup of difference

YOU WILL NEED: scales or a balance; a cup; 2 substances to weigh and a pencil.

How much difference can there be in the weight of one cupful of different substances?

● First of all find a cup, weigh it and write down its weight.

Cup = ... grams

● Now find something that you can put in the cup which you and your partner think is really light and something which you think is really heavy. Write down their names.

● Weigh them both in the cup. (Both things must fill the cup.)

● Work out their weights and write them down.

Light thing	Heavy thing
....	....
.................grams	.... grams

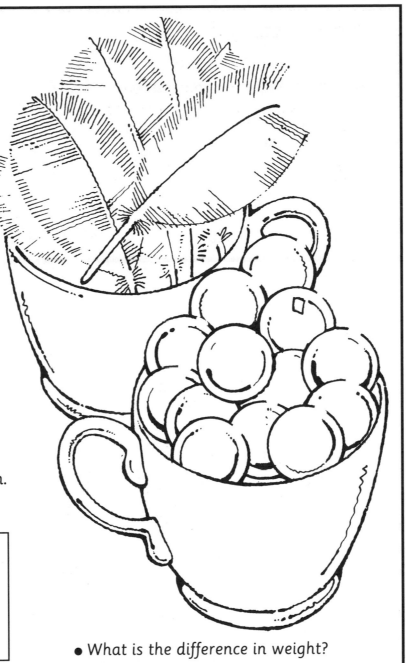

● What is the difference in weight?

Dear Parent or Carer

Give your child time to experiment with different substances before choosing. The weights of many substances can be quite surprising!

_____and
child

_____
helper(s)

_____

did this activity together

_____and

child

_____

helper(s)

_____

did this activity together

Time to play

What happens when on a Saturday?

● Make a timeline of all the things you
do on Saturday.

● First of all, make a list of each hour
with a space beside it:

8.00 ....

9.00 ....

and so on.

● Now write or draw what you were
doing at that time. If possible, write
precise times on your timeline, for
example 'At 10.30 I went shopping.'

● Keep your timeline somewhere
handy like on the kitchen table,
so that you do not forget to fill it in!

impact MATHS HOMEWORK

Record breakers

How quick or slow are you? Not at running or jumping or anything like that, but at ordinary things in life like dressing, washing, getting ready for school and – yes – tidying up!

● Ask someone to time you doing 3 routine things, such as dressing, washing and getting ready for school.

● Write down your times in the table below.

name of event	time in minutes

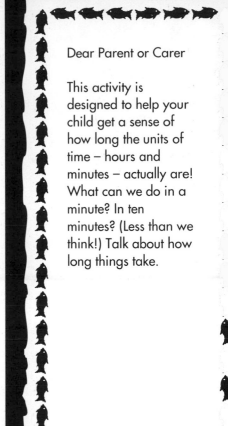

Dear Parent or Carer

This activity is designed to help your child get a sense of how long the units of time – hours and minutes – actually are! What can we do in a minute? In ten minutes? (Less than we think!) Talk about how long things take.

_____and

child

_____

helper(s)

_____

did this activity together

_____and

child

_____

helper(s)

_____

did this activity together

Timing times

YOU WILL NEED: a counter for each player; a dice and someone to play with.

● Take it in turns to throw the dice. Move that many clock faces along the track.

● Look at the space you stop on. You must read out loud the time on that space, and write the same time as a digital display, so half past four would be written 4.30.

● If you are right, you stay on that space. If not, move back 3 spaces!

● The first player to the end is the winner.

impact MATHS HOMEWORK

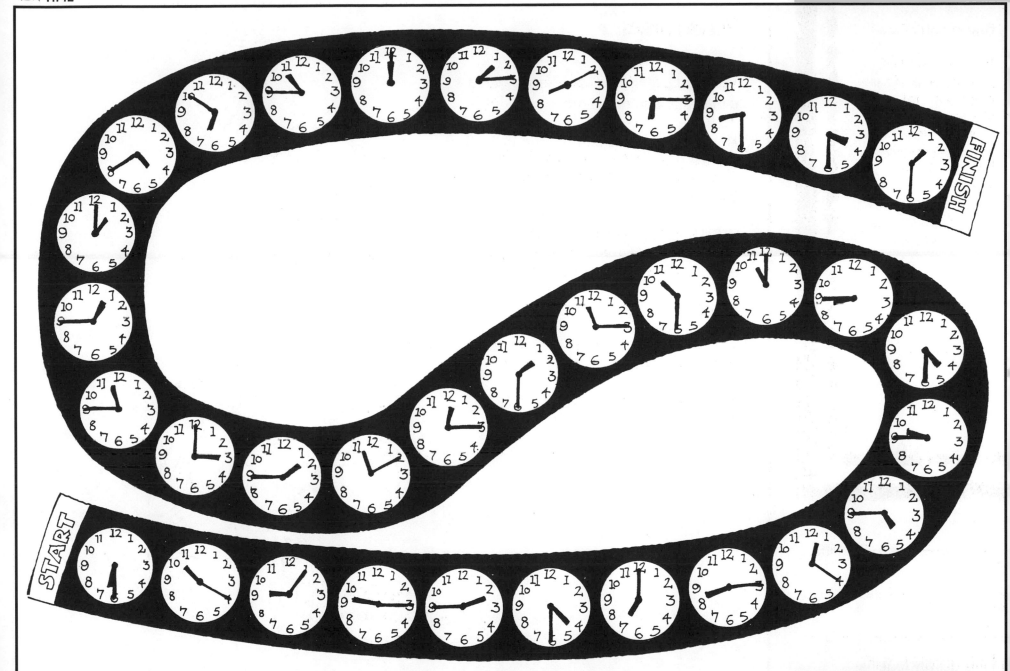

I.M. MARSH LIBRARY LIVERPOOL L17 6BD
TEL. 0151 231 5216/5299

Dear Parent or Carer

This activity is designed to help your child get a sense of how long the units of time – hours and minutes – actually are. What can we do in a minute? In ten minutes? (Less than we think!) Talk about how long things take.

_____and

child

_____

helper(s)

_____

did this activity together

All in a minute

YOU WILL NEED: a minute timer; a pencil; a ball and a dice.

How many things can you do in 1 minute?

● How many times can you:

WRITE YOUR NAME? (Just first name)

HOP UP AND DOWN ON ONE LEG?

THROW AND CATCH A BALL? (It doesn't count if you don't catch it!)

DRAW A FACE?

CLAP YOUR HANDS?

THROW A 6 ON THE DICE?

impact MATHS HOMEWORK

In the blink of an eye

YOU WILL NEED: a ball; a book and a pencil.

How long does it take you to:

WRITE OUT A TIMES TABLE (not 1 or 2!)?

COUNT UP TO 100?

WRITE A 2 LINE POEM?

THROW AND CATCH A BALL 10 TIMES?

READ A PAGE OF YOUR BOOK?

● Ask someone patient to time you doing all these things.

Dear Parent or Carer

This activity is designed to help your child get a sense of how long the units of time – hours and minutes – actually are. What can we do in a minute? In ten minutes? (Less than we think!) Talk about how long things take.

_____and

child

_____

helper(s)

_____

did this activity together

Dear Parent or Carer

It is true that time seems longer if you are waiting or bored and seems to fly if you are having fun! Children have to realise that when we measure time, it doesn't make any difference what you are doing!

_____and

child

_____

helper(s)

_____

did this activity together

TV watch

YOU WILL NEED: a clock or watch and a pencil.

● When you are having fun, time flies past! How long do you actually spend doing one of the following:

WATCHING YOUR FAVOURITE TV PROGRAMME?

READING A CHAPTER OF YOUR FAVOURITE BOOK?

LISTENING TO YOUR FAVOURITE TAPE/ CD/RECORD?

● Ask someone patient and accurate to time you while you do one of these.

● Write down the time when you start

....

● Write down the time when you finish

....

● How long did you take?

.... **minutes**

impact MATHS HOMEWORK

A watched clock

- Find a clock in your house that is reliable!

- Draw it and the time it says, then go and see if you can find another clock in your house. It doesn't matter if it is a digital clock. If you can't find one, does someone have a watch?

- Draw their watch or the other clock. Draw the time it says. How different is it from the first one?

Dear Parent or Carer

This activity is intended to help your child find the difference between two times. This is very useful when using timetables and working out problems to do with starting and finishing times.

_____and

child

_____

helper(s)

_____

did this activity together

Dear Parent or Carer

This activity helps children to remember and recognise the order of the months of the year. Please help your child to memorise these.

_____and

child

_____

helper(s)

_____

did this activity together

Year clock

● Write in 2 events for each month on this year clock. (You may have to turn the paper round.)

● Write the dates in the month when they happen.

You could put on birthdays, football matches, anniversaries, holiday dates...

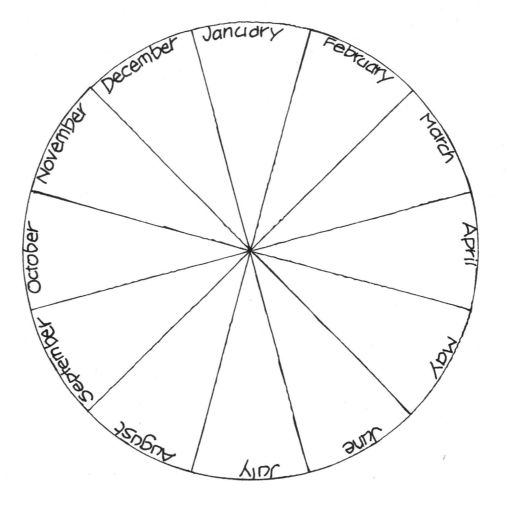

impact MATHS HOMEWORK

Chinese year signs

Chinese years are designated by animals in the following order:

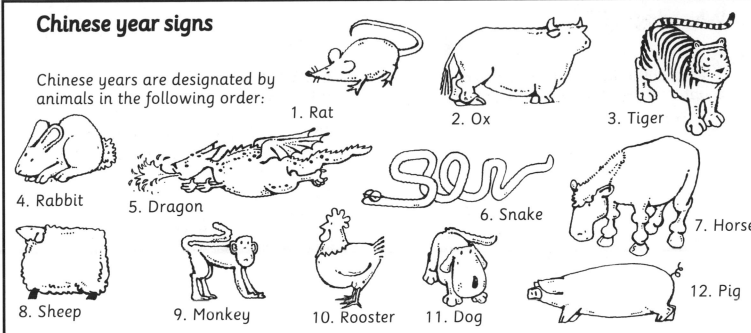

1. Rat
2. Ox
3. Tiger
4. Rabbit
5. Dragon
6. Snake
7. Horse
8. Sheep
9. Monkey
10. Rooster
11. Dog
12. Pig

● Find out the year each member of your family was born. Include some friends too if you like!

● Now work out which animal they are. NB. The year of the rat fell in 1948, 1960, 1972 and 1984. You should be able to work out the rest from this! If a person's birthday is before February 14 they count as the previous year's animal.

● Write their year of birth and animal name in the table, and bring your lists into school.

person	date of birth	Chinese year

Dear Parent or Carer

This activity is good fun and helps to learn to count in years. It may help if your child only looks at the last two figures of the year number.

_____and

child

_____

helper(s)

_____

did this activity together

_____and

child

_____

helper(s)

_____

did this activity together

What day is it?

The difficult thing about the way we count time is that the 2nd of the month might be on a different day each month!

● Look at this year's calendar. Working with a partner can you find out:

Which day of the week your birthday is on?

Whether you will be at school on your birthday?

Whether, if you are given your pocket money on a Saturday, you will get more in some months than others?

Which months you will get more?

Which day of the week Christmas Day is this year?

Which day of the week August bank holiday falls on?

Which day is the last day of the year?

Which day is fireworks day?

Which day is Halloween?

impact MATHS HOMEWORK

Calendar count up

The calendar varies from year to year, for example, some years have more days than others, some years begin on a Monday, some on a Tuesday, and so on.

● Study the calendar for this year with your partner.

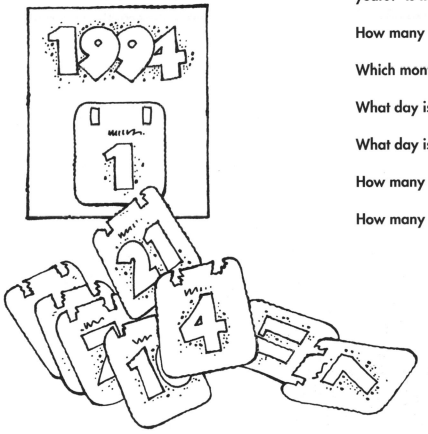

● Write down the year, then answer the following questions.

Year . . . .

How many Sundays are there in March?

Which date only comes round every four years? Is it there this year?

How many months start on a Monday?

Which months end on a Saturday?

What day is Christmas Day?

What day is your birthday?

How many weekdays are there in December?

How many weekends are there in August?

Dear Parent or Carer

This activity will help your child to read and understand how a calendar works. It also reinforces knowledge of the days of the week and the months of the year. Please talk about the calendar with your child.

_____and

child

_____

helper(s)

_____

did this activity together

_____and

child

_____

helper(s)

_____

did this activity together

Rock around the clock

What times of the day do you eat?

How much time do you spend eating?

● Today, every time you have something to eat make a note of the time you start and the time you finish.

● Keep a list of all your eating times – you do not have to write down what you eat, just when!

time I started eating	time I finished eating

impact MATHS HOMEWORK

Ticking clocks

YOU WILL NEED: a dice, a pencil and
a big hand for the clock made of card.

Use the clock picture on the right to play
a game.

● Start with the big hand pointing at
12.

● Take it in turns to throw the dice.

If you throw a 5 move the big hand
round the clock 1 space.

When you throw a different number –
not a 5 – add it to your score each turn.
(So, if you throw a 2 in your first turn,
you have a score of 2. If you throw a 6
in your second turn, you have a score of
8...)

● Keep playing until you have thrown
enough 5s for the big hand to reach the
12. Add up your scores. The player with
the lowest score wins!

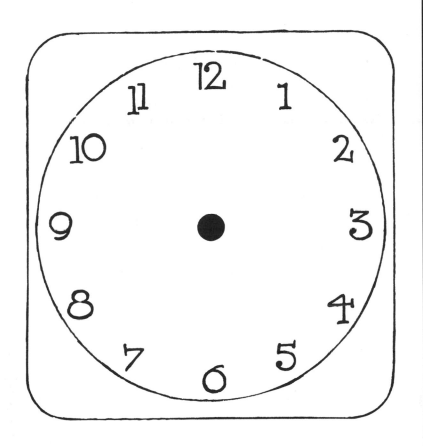

Dear Parent or Carer

This activity will help
your child to tell the
time. Discuss why you
can only move when
you throw a five and
the movement of the
hour hand in relation
to the minute hand.
Try counting in fives
around the clock. This
helps with digital time
telling.

_____and

child

_____

helper(s)

_____

did this activity together

impact MATHS HOMEWORK

Second time

YOU WILL NEED: a piece of string that is exactly 1 metre long, and a small heavy thing to use as a weight to hang on the end (a teaspoon would do!).

You are going to make something to time things accurately.

● Tie the weight to one end of your piece of string and tie the other end to something fixed so that it can swing freely.

● Time someone in your house (count the number of swings) while they do the following things:

Put on their coat

Put on their shoes

Write their name four times

Eat a slice of bread!

● Write down how many swings for each one.

● Now ask someone to time you doing the same things!

impact MATHS HOMEWORK

Judge of time

YOU WILL NEED: a watch with a second hand and a pencil.

Are you a good judge of time? Can you estimate when one minute has passed?

● Ask someone to help you. They will need a watch with a second hand or a timer.

● When they say, 'Start' you must tell them when you think 1 minute has passed.

● Write down how long it was really! (For example: If you say 'Now' and only 40 seconds had passed, you write 40 seconds.)

● Now let them take a turn and you time them. How long was their guess? Write it down.

● Try this with as many people as you can. Who is the closest?

name	guess

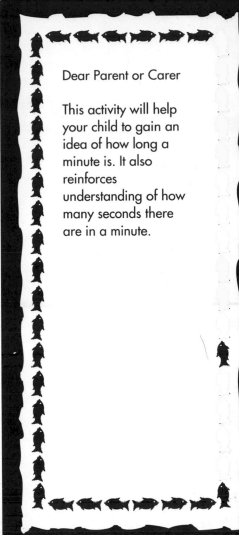

Dear Parent or Carer

This activity will help your child to gain an idea of how long a minute is. It also reinforces understanding of how many seconds there are in a minute.

_____and
child

_____
helper(s)

_____
did this activity together

Dear Parent or Carer

This activity will help
your child to think
about different lengths
of time and how long
quite ordinary
household tasks take.
It will help to show
which units of time are
appropriate for
measuring which time
intervals.

_____and

child

_____

helper(s)

_____

did this activity together

Freezing cold

YOU WILL NEED: a fridge with a freezer;
water; juice; food colouring; sugar or
salt and a pencil.

● Make some unusual ice cubes.

● You could use:

water and juice

or water and colouring

or water and sugar

or water and salt.

● Try to make several different types.

● How long do they each take to freeze?
(You will need to check them at regular
intervals.)

● Design a chart to record the times.

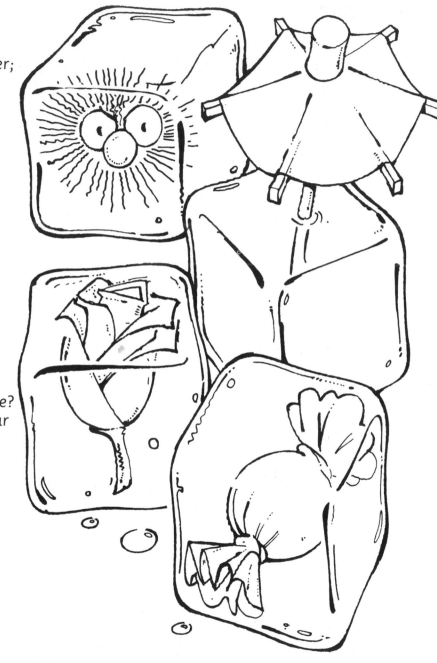

impact MATHS HOMEWORK

Heartbeat

YOU WILL NEED: a watch with a second hand and a pencil.

You have an in-built ticker – your heart!

This beat can be felt as your pulse.

How many times does your heart beat each minute?

● First of all find your pulse – it can be felt in your neck or wrist.

● Now ask someone to help you count it. (They time you for one minute and you count the number of beats.)

● Write down the number. In the first heart shape below.

● Now ask them to time you for 6 seconds while you count heartbeats.

● Write down the number in the second heart shape.

● Multiply this by 10 (10 x number of seconds = 1 minute). Is the answer the same?

Dear Parent or Carer

This activity will help to practise the skills of timing and estimating time intervals. Involve your child in both the taking of the pulse and the timing if you can. Help to be as accurate as possible.

_____and

child

_____

helper(s)

_____

did this activity together

Dear Parent or Carer

This activity will help to practise timing intervals. Help your child to look at a clock and to decide what time it is. How long has passed when the item is dry?

_____and

child

_____

helper(s)

_____

did this activity together

Washing times

● Ask someone at home if you can carry out an experiment when they next do the washing. Tell them it will not hurt the clothes!

● Choose several articles of clothing that are made of different fabrics and list them in the chart below.

● When the items are washed, hang them up to dry and note down the time.

● How long does it take each one to dry? You will need to check at regular intervals.

● Record the times in the chart.

article	how long

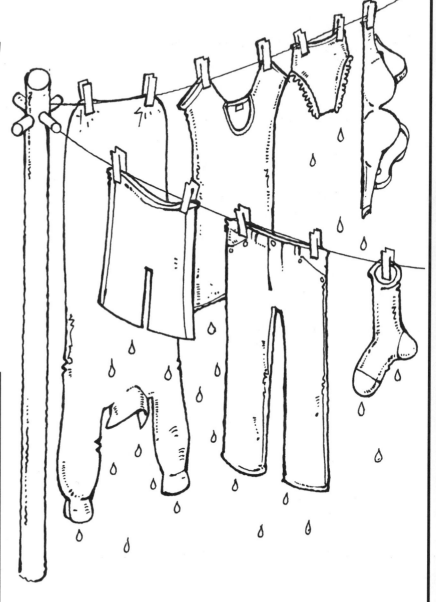

impact MATHS HOMEWORK

Life times

YOU WILL NEED: scissors and a pencil.

● How many years have you lived?

● Cut out a strip that contains that number of squares from the squares below. Write your name on it.

● Now ask a grown-up at home how many years they have lived.

● Cut out a strip that contains that many squares. Write their name on that.

● How many times will your strip fit on to their strip? Write down your answer.

It fits .... times

(You may have to use halves!)

This is how many times older than you they are.

● If you like, do this for someone else in your home.

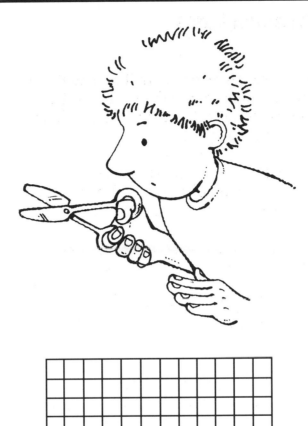

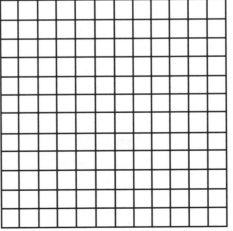

Dear Parent or Carer

This activity is designed to help children to relate their age to other people's lifetimes. Many small children have no sense of adults and children's relative ages. They often think that Mum is older than Gran!

_____and

child

_____

helper(s)

_____

did this activity together

_____and

child

_____

helper(s)

_____

did this activity together

Family history

● Make a family history time-track for your family.

● Draw a long track, starting in the year when your oldest parent was born and progressing to the year 2000. Write the years on the track. For example: 1950, 1951, 1952, 1953... and so on.

● Mark the leap years on your track and all the events of importance to your family.

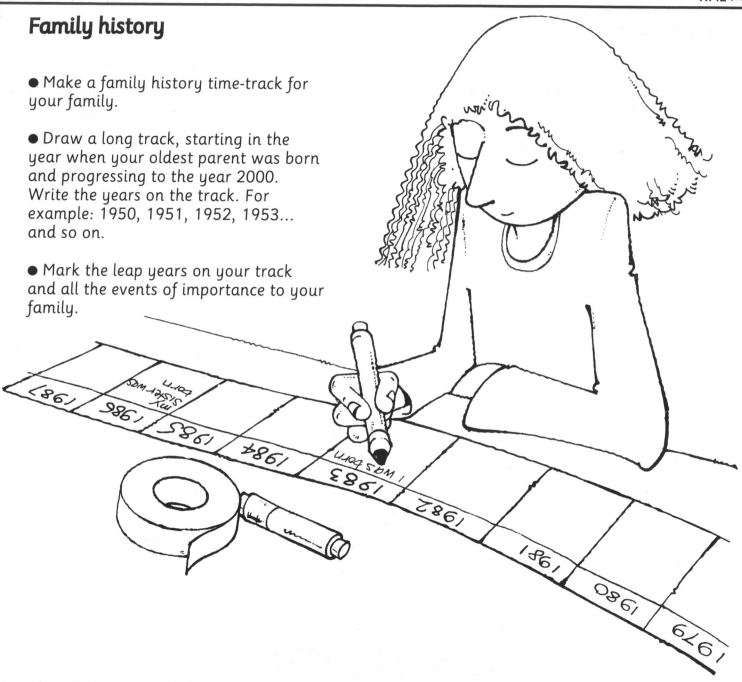

impact MATHS HOMEWORK

Christmas time

YOU WILL NEED: someone clever to help you – and lots of patience.

Lola lives in Victoria, Australia. One Christmas she travels to see her family in Los Angeles (USA). She leaves her home on Christmas Day and manages to organise things so that she gets three Christmas dinners – all of them eaten at dinner time on Christmas Day.

How does she do this?

Dear Parent or Carer

It is worth remembering two things! First, Lola crosses the International Date Line. Second, she eats on the plane! Also it takes about 16 hours to fly from Melbourne to Los Angeles and America is six hours behind Australia in time. This activity will help your child to think about the 24 hour clock.

_____and

child

_____

helper(s)

_____

did this activity together

impact MATHS HOMEWORK

_____and

child

_____

helper(s)

_____

did this activity together

TV survey

YOU WILL NEED: a newspaper, a pencil and paper and the accompanying sheet.

● Look at the TV page of a newspaper.

● How much news and current affairs is broadcast on each channel? Look at the space for each channel on the accompanying sheet and write down all the news or current affairs programmes. Write down how long each one is.

● Add up the total time for each channel.

● Now work out the total time each channel is on the air during the day.

● Do the same for comedy programmes.

impact MATHS HOMEWORK

BBC 1

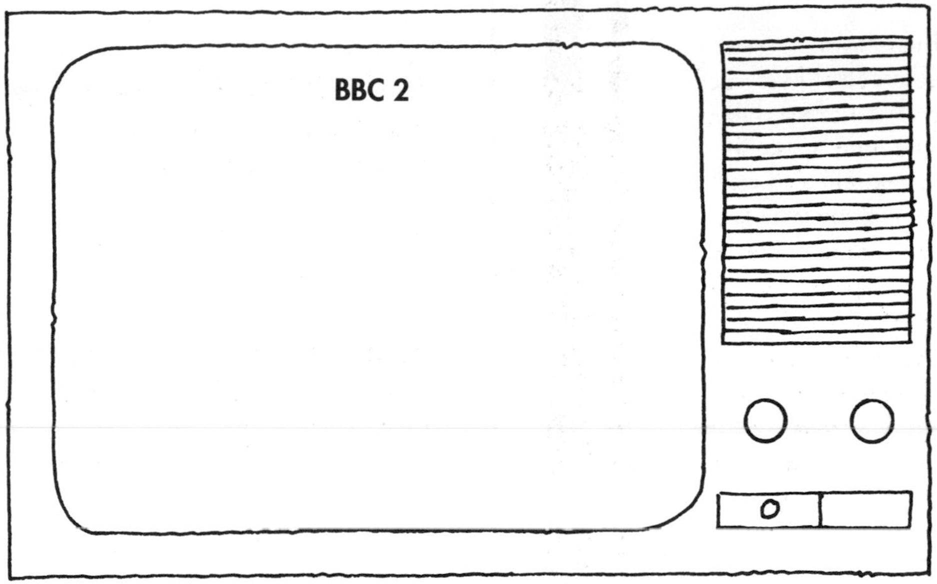

BBC 2

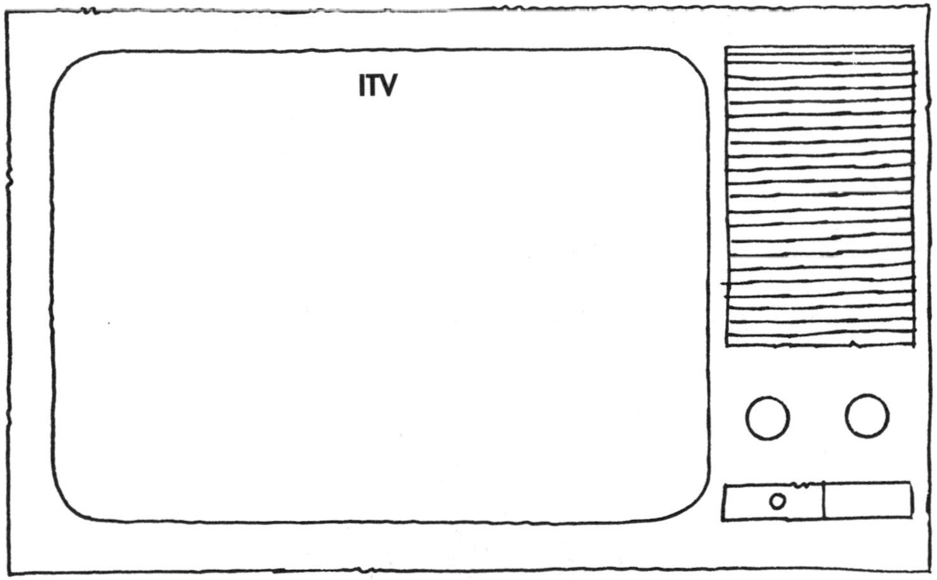

ITV

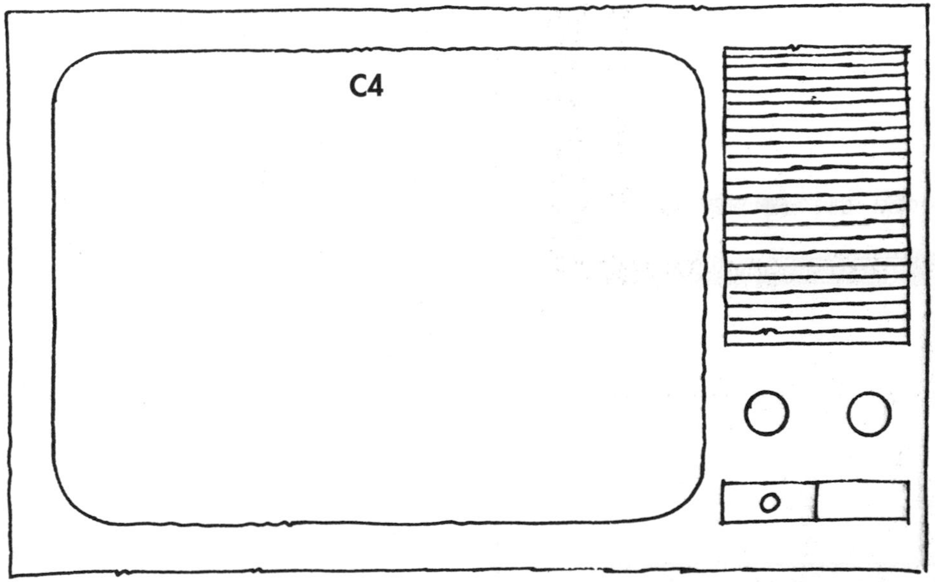

C4

_____and

child

_____

helper(s)

_____

did this activity together

Time leaks

YOU WILL NEED: salt or sugar; a plate and scissors.

● Make or find a container that holds 1 litre.

● Cut it, or change it, so that its contents will leak out in exactly 1 minute! Be cautious – don't cut until you have thought about it.

● Use salt or sugar to test it out.

● Be careful to let it leak on to a clean plate so that you do not waste the salt/sugar.

impact MATHS HOMEWORK

Seasonal times

There are 4 seasons in the year.

In each season there is a certain amount of darkness and a certain amount of light.

● Talk to someone in your home about what time it gets light and what time it gets dark at different times of year and try to work out how many hours of darkness there are in each season.

● Make a graph or chart to display this information.

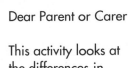

Dear Parent or Carer

This activity looks at the differences in hours of darkness during summer and winter. Your child will need to estimate, using the fact that the day is always 24 hours long, and to think about how to represent the results.

_____and

child

_____

helper(s)

_____

did this activity together

_____and

child

_____

helper(s)

_____

did this activity together

Century lifetimes

● How many years have you been alive?

● How many of your lifetimes (up until now!) will fit into a century?

● How many of your mum or dad or brother or sister's lifetimes will fit into a century?

● Work this out for as many people as you can. Write down their ages, and how many of their lifetimes will fit into a century in each case.

● Do you, or does anyone in your family, know someone who lived to be 100 years old?

name	lifetimes in a century

impact MATHS HOMEWORK

Millions of seconds

YOU WILL NEED: a calculator to work out the answers.

● How many hours old are you?

● How many minutes?

● How many seconds?

● Write down your answers.

● When you have worked this out, estimate how many seconds old you think a grown-up you know is!

● Check your estimates!

How many hours old are you?

How many minutes?

How many seconds?

_____and

child

_____

helper(s)

_____

did this activity together

Dear Parent or Carer

This activity is intended to make sure that children are confident about which coin is which and the relative values of each. It will also practise addition skills.

Coin collect

YOU WILL NEED: an example of each coin of the realm and a pencil.

● Take it in turns to play.

● Choose a coin from the pile to spin or toss in the air.

If it lands heads you may keep it.

If it lands tails put it back!

● Keep taking it in turns to play until there are no more coins!

● Count up your money. This is your score. Write it down.

● The player with the score nearest to 90p wins.

● Play this game 3 times.

_____and

child

_____

helper(s)

_____

did this activity together

impact MATHS HOMEWORK

Coin threesome

Dear Parent or Carer

This activity is designed to reinforce your child's knowledge not only of what our coins look like, but of their value. Talk about what each coin will buy. How much is it worth?

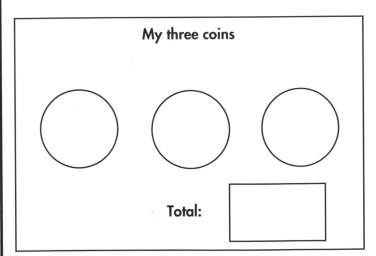

My three coins

○ ○ ○

Total: ☐

● Choose 3 different coins.

● Write their values in the circles on the left, then add them up. How much do they make? Write down your answer.

● Now think of something that you could buy with just that amount of money. It must be something that you would like to have!

● Draw it on the back of this sheet.

_____and

child

_____

helper(s)

_____

did this activity together

Change for 50p

YOU WILL NEED: a handful of coins;
a pencil and paper and a pack of cards
with the face cards removed.

● Place the cards in a pile, face down.

● Take it in turns to collect 3 cards from
the pile.

● Add up their values. This is the
amount of money you have.

● How much change would you have if
you were to spend this amount using a
50p coin? Work it out and write down
the answer. This is your score. Take
that amount from the pile of money.

● Keep playing until one player has a
score that is over £2.00. They win!

_____and

child

_____

helper(s)

_____

did this activity together

impact MATHS HOMEWORK

Big money

It is surprising how expensive some small things are and how cheap some which are large can be!

They say money can't buy you love, but it also doesn't always buy size!

● Talk to someone in your home and see if you can think of something that is very large and not very expensive, and something that is very small and very expensive.

● Draw the 2 things on a piece of paper or the back of this sheet and write the price you think they would cost beside them.

Dear Parent or Carer

This activity is designed to help your child think about the notion of value. What is it that makes some things expensive, and other things cheap? Which things are expensive and which are cheap? Talk about this with your child.

_____and

child

_____

helper(s)

_____

did this activity together

_____and

child

_____

helper(s)

_____

did this activity together

Measuring

Noteworthy

● Ask someone if you can look at a £5 or a £10 note. They can help you do this activity.

● Study the note with some care. How many centimetres long, and how many centimetres wide is it?

● What does it have written and drawn on it? Write the measurements and draw the design on a piece of paper or the back of this sheet.

● Now discuss the sorts of thing that you could buy with this note (and no more!). Colour in the value of your note on the table below then write one or more things under each section of the table (which add up to the value of the note).

	food	toys	drinks	outings/treats!
£5				
£10				

impact MATHS HOMEWORK

Score of coins

YOU WILL NEED: a handful of coins, including at least one of each type except £1; a dice and paper and a pencil for each player.

● Take it in turns to throw the dice and write down your score.

If it is a number which is also a coin, for example 2 = a 2p coin, take that coin. If it isn't, wait for your next turn and throw the dice again.

● Add the number thrown to your score and write it down. If your score now totals a number which is also a coin, take that coin.

● Keep playing in this way until your score reaches over 50. You may then start again from 0.

● The first player to collect an amount of coins over 25p is the winner.

Dear Parent or Carer

This activity will help your child to think about how much each coin is worth and also to practise some quick mental addition and keep a running score. The more fun you make the game, the more maths your child will do!

_____and
child

_____
helper(s)

_____

did this activity together

_____and

child

_____

helper(s)

_____

did this activity together

Measuring

Change for £1

YOU WILL NEED: a handful of coins; a dice and a pencil and paper.

● Take it in turns to throw the dice 3 times.

● Add up your scores.

● If you were spending this amount, what change would you have from £1? Work out the answer and write it down.

● Keep playing until you have had 6 turns each then add up your answers.

● The player with the highest total is the winner.

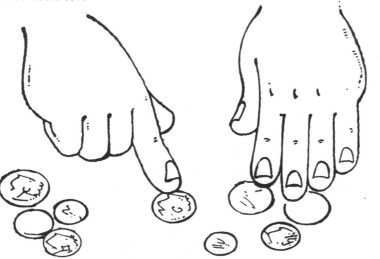

score	change from £1
total	

player 1

score	change from £1
total	

player 2

Easy change

In India and other countries in Asia, men cycle huge tricycles which can carry passengers! If you were to ride one of these here in Britain what sort of fare would you charge?

You will need to make sure that the fare you charge is an amount of money which makes it easy to give change.

What coins would be used to pay?

Which coins would you have to carry to give change?

The fare would also need to be lower than the bus fare but as much as you think people would be prepared to pay!

● Talk to someone in your home and decide what you think a reasonable fare would be.

● Write it down – and give your reasons!

NOTE: You might want to set the fare according to the distance. You would not accept passengers who wanted to go more than 3 or 4 miles!

Dear Parent or Carer

This activity will make your child think about prices and how much it costs to travel around. It is important that we teach children about how much things cost, and how much we have to pay for things even when at the moment they may not have to deal with such matters on a daily basis.

_____and

child

_____

helper(s)

_____

did this activity together

impact MATHS HOMEWORK

Dear Parent or Carer

This activity is intended to help your child to round up and round down numbers. This is an important skill and one needed both mathematically speaking and in everyday life!

_____and

child

_____

helper(s)

_____

did this activity together

Measuring

Close approximation

YOU WILL NEED: a pen and a shopping receipt – with about 10 or 15 items on it. (It could have more than this – but you will only need to use that many.)

● Write down all the amounts.

● Now write the amount rounded up or down to the nearest 10p beside them.
For example: 38p becomes 40p
                      £1.23 becomes £1.20

● Add up both lists.

● Are the totals about the same? Which one is more?

● Would this be a satisfactory way of working out how much you were going to spend in a supermarket as you go round?

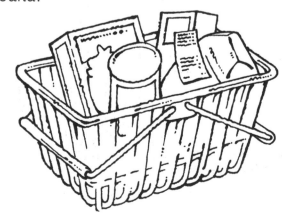

amount	amount rounded up/down
Total:	

Price wise

● Ask someone to take you with them when they go shopping. Find 3 things that are all the same weight – such as jams, canned drinks, cheeses....

● Write down the name of each item and its price in order (from highest to lowest).

● Which one do you think is the best value? Why?

item	price

Dear Parent or Carer

This activity is designed to help your child realise the worth of different things and to explore the notion of 'value for money'. It is important that we teach children about how much things cost, even if at the moment they may not have to deal with such matters on a daily basis.

_____and

child

_____

helper(s)

_____

did this activity together

Biscuit value

● Find a packet of biscuits which you like. (It could be sweet or cheese biscuits, crispbread, or anything similar.)

● How much does it cost?

● How many biscuits are there in the packet?

● Work out how much each biscuit costs!

● Write down your answers.

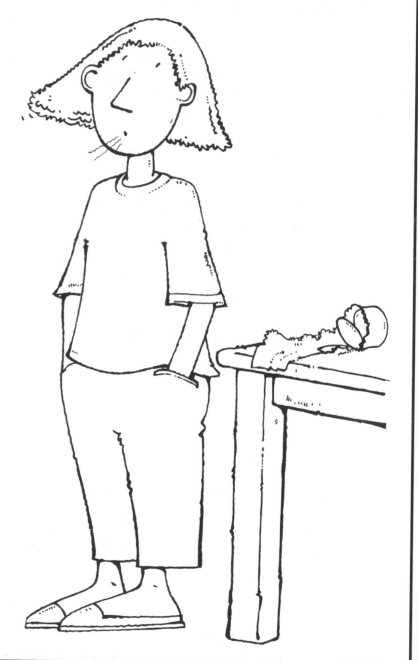

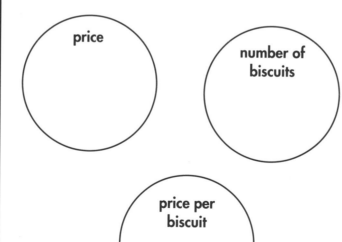

price

number of biscuits

price per biscuit

Dear Parent or Carer

For this activity your child will need to practise division in a practical setting, and think about the cost of these items. This is helpful when we are dealing, not just with the arithmetical skills involved in working with money, but with the 'real life' skills involved in shopping!

_____and

child

_____

helper(s)

did this activity together

Measuring

Shopping basket survey

Every month someone somewhere works out how much the basic cost of living has risen this month. You are going to do something similar!

● Work out which 20 items you think are the MOST ESSENTIAL things for a family to buy on a weekly basis. Obviously bread might be one of them, but would butter or margarine? Would meat? Which vegetables would be?

● Discuss this with your family and make a list of 20 items.

● Put the price beside each one, then total up the cost.

item	price
total	

Dear Parent or Carer

This activity requires your child to do a lot of arithmetic *and* to think about the cost of living! It is important that we teach children about how much things cost, and how much we have to pay for things even when at the moment they may not have to deal with such matters on a daily basis.

_____and

child

_____

helper(s)

_____

did this activity together

impact MATHS HOMEWORK

_____and

child

_____

helper(s)

_____

did this activity together

Measuring

How much do I need?

Imagine that your family has said that they will give you an allowance.

They are going to house you and feed you but everything else that you need – clothes, toys, books, travel (not to school!), films and anything else you will have to pay for yourself.

They have agreed an allowance of £10 per month.

● How will you plan to spend this?

● How much will go on clothes? Shoes? Travel?

● It will help if you talk to whoever buys your clothes and shoes about how much it costs.

● Work out a satisfactory spending plan. Write down the details.

Realm count up

If you had one of every single coin and note of the realm which is legal currency, how much money would you have?

● Ask as many people as you can find to guess. They mustn't work it out – just guess!

● Make a list of their names and write down their guesses.

● Now work it out. Who was closest?

name	guess

Dear Parent or Carer

This activity is immense fun! Ask as many of your friends, relations (and enemies!) to try it as you can. There is more skill than you think involved in the estimate!

_____and

child

_____

helper(s)

_____

did this activity together

_____and

child

_____

helper(s)

'd this activity together

Measuring

Rich uncle

A rich uncle has returned from abroad. He puts his hand in his pocket and pulls out a handful of coins.

'These are all for you!' he says.

You cannot believe your luck!

'But,' he goes on, 'You have to work for it!'

'Thought it was too good to be true,' you mutter.

'You have to tell me which coins I am holding. But I'll make it easy for you. I have £7.28 in all. I am holding 15 coins. Five are identical. I have one coin in my hand which is half the value of another coin, of which I have only three. I have three 50ps. Which other coins am I holding?'

● Can you earn the money? Write down the coins you think he is holding.

How much is a cornflake?

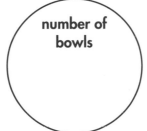

number of bowls

price

price of 1 bowl

Have you ever wondered how much a bowl of your favourite cereal costs? No? That's because you probably haven't had to pay for it yourself!

● First of all, find a packet of your favourite breakfast cereal.

● What does it cost? Write down the price.

● Now work out how many bowls of cereal it contains.

● How much does 1 bowl cost?

● Can you calculate the cost of 1 piece of cereal?

Dear Parent or Carer

This activity involves a great deal of mathematical thinking in order to sort out a suitable strategy. It will also involve some fine judgements – help your child with these by talking through the activity.

_____and

child

_____

helper(s)

_____

did this activity together

impact MATHS HOMEWORK

Dear Parent or Carer

This activity makes a lovely trick question for children to try on unsuspecting friends and relations! How many can guess the answer? Help your child to work out how many figures in one billion.

_____and

child

_____

helper(s)

_____

this activity together

Measuring

Tricky question

● Can you puzzle this out?

What costs 10p for one?
20p for ten?
30p for one hundred?
40p for one thousand?

● Think really hard! The information on this page may give you a clue.

● When you have worked it out, calculate how much it would cost to buy one billion (NB One billion is one million million!)

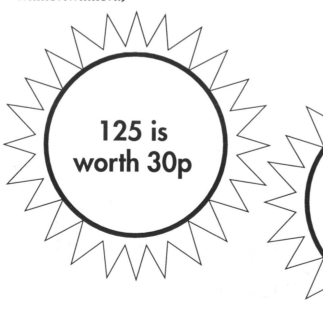

8 is worth 10p

58 is worth 20p

125 is worth 30p

1342 is worth 40p

Answer: Numerals! For example: If I buy 24 it will cost me 10p for the '2' and 10p for the '4', 20p in all.

Body temperatures

Find a way to take your temperature.

● Ask around to see if anyone you know has a thermometer for taking a person's temperature.

● Look at it carefully.

● What units is it using? Write down their name.

....

● What is the scale? It goes from

.... to ....

● Take your temperature. What is it?

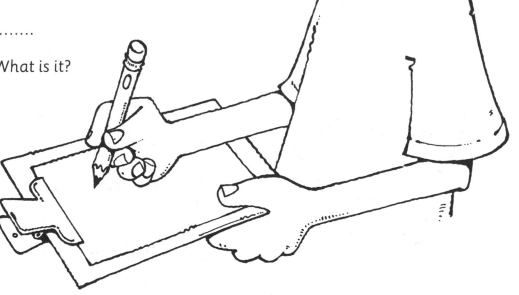

Dear Parent or Carer

This activity will help your child to master the idea of a scale in relation to temperature. We shall be looking at the possible units with which we measure temperature nowadays, and which ones are commonly used for which purposes.

_____and

child

_____

helper(s)

_____

did this activity together

Dear Parent or Carer

This activity introduces the different units used for measuring temperatures nowadays. We shall be looking at temperature scales in class, and considering what happens when a temperature becomes a negative number!

_____ and

child

_____

helper(s)

d this activity together

Measuring

Weather search

YOU WILL NEED: to listen to the weather forecast on the TV or radio twice. One time should be during the day – preferably the morning; one time should be during the evening.

● Listen out for the temperatures on the weather forecast.

● Write down the temperature in your area during the day.

● Write down the expected temperature in your area at night.

● What units are these temperatures given in?

● What is the difference between the 2 temperatures?

● Can you say what the temperature would be if the weather is freezing?

Scottish National Guidelines Mathematics 5–14

Number, Money and Measurement

Measure and Estimate

Level C – Measure in standard units: weight (accuracy extended to include 20g weights); volume and area. Estimate length and height in easily handled standard units. Select appropriate measuring devices and units for length. Read scales on measuring devices to the nearest graduation where the value of an intermediate graduation may need to be deduced. Realise that weight and area can be conserved when shape changes.

Level D – Measure in standard units: length; weight; volume; area and temperature. Estimate small weights, areas and volumes in easily handled standard units. Recognise when kilometres are appropriate. Select appropriate measuring devices and units for weight. Be aware of common Imperial units in appropriate practical applications.

Level E – Measure and draw using standard units. Estimate measurements: areas in square metres, small lengths in millimetres, larger lengths in metres. Work with square kilometre, hectare, tonne when appropriate. Read scales on measuring devices including estimating between graduations. Realise that volume can be conserved when shape changes

Time

Level C – Work with time: use 12 hour times for simple timetables; conventions for recording time; work with hours and minutes; use calendars.

Level D – Work with time: use 24-hour times with 12-hour times; calculate duration in hours/minutes, mentally if possible; time activities in seconds with a stopwatch; calculate speeds.

Level E – Time activities with a digital stopwatch in seconds, tenths, hundredths.

Northern Ireland Programme of Study for Mathematics at Key Stage 2

Measures

Pupils should have opportunities to:
a develop skills in estimation of length, 'weight', volume/capacity, time, area and temperature through practical activities, using metric units where appropriate;
b develop the language associated with a wider range of metric units and be confident with the terms metre, gram and litre, and their relevant prefixes of kilo, centi, milli;
c appreciate important ideas about measurement including the continuousmeasurement and the need for appropriate accuracy;
d choose and use appropriate metric units and measuring instruments in a variety of situations, interpreting numbers on a range of measuring instruments;
e understand the relationship between units; convert from one metric unit to another; use the four operations to solve problems, working with up to three decimal places, where appropriate;
f know the Imperial units still in common use including foot, yard, mile, pound and pint;
g understand and use negative numbers in context;
h understand the concept of perimeter and calculate the perimeter of simple shapes; find areas by counting squares and volumes by counting cubes; calculate areas and volumes of simple shapes in two and three dimensions;
i understand and use scale in the context of simple maps/drawings;
j know the units of measurement of time and the relationship between them;
k recognise times on the analogue clock, including the hour, half and quarter hours, five minute intervals and one minute intervals; understand the relationship between the 12 and 24-hour clocks including am and pm; read analogue and digital displays and understand the relationship between them; use timetables involving the 24-hour clock and perform simple calculations related to timetables;
l know the months of the year; explore calendar patterns

Money

Pupils should have opportunities to:
a understand and use the conventional way of recording money; use the four operations to solve problems;
b estimate and approximate to gain a feeling for the size of a solution to a problem before carrying out a calculation;
c interpret a calculator display in relation to money.